MANDATORY

NICK GOSS

FOR EVERY HARDWORKING DAD WHO LOOKS FOR-
WARD TO HIS CUP OF BLACK COFFEE ON CHRISTMAS
MORNING.

Preface

The office Christmas party in Mandatory is not altogether fictional. It was largely inspired by a holiday party at the company I work full-time for. Many of the events and conversations actually happened, while others are completely made up. The characters are largely based on actual coworkers of mine, though names, genders, races, etc. have been changed. Very few of the characters and events in the book were made up. I'll leave it up to you to guess what's real and what's not.

It is my hope that some of the good old-fashioned sentiment of the holiday seeps into your heart as you read, and that you will not neglect the most blessed season of the entire year. In light of the darkest political time in our country's history, I believe that we need Christmas *now* more than ever.

My belief is that what we call the 'spirit of Christmas' is in fact the one thing that can heal a very politically divided country. Let 'peace on earth, good will toward men' be your mantra this season. And when the new year rolls around and the decorations are stowed away in the attic, I hope that you will come along with me as I, like the reformed Scrooge, pledge to "honor Christmas in my heart, and try to keep it all the year."

1

Attendance was mandatory. The company-wide email made it very clear. There would be no opting out of the Blackstone & Harding office Christmas party. Exceptions were only made for those whose time off requests had been approved at least two months in advance. For those who missed that deadline, they had no choice but to be at work on December the 20th. They were expected to spend their entire afternoon that day from noon to five o'clock participating in the festivities. Luther was one of those unfortunate souls who missed the time off request deadline. He also, for his own perfectly justifiable reasons, hated Christmas.

He scanned the email for the fine print. It clearly ordered that nobody would be allowed to sneak back to their desks during the festivities. No work was to be done that afternoon, so laptops and company cell phones would not be permitted at the party. Nobody would be allowed to leave the party early to 'beat the traffic.' The length of one's commute home, nor the weather forecast, which was looking more ominous by the day, would have any bearing on the mandate to attend. There would be no shirking the holiday frivolities. It was ironclad.

I like everything about Jesus except Christmas, Luther thought, *unlike some of the purple-haired liberals in human resources. They love everything about Christmas except Jesus.* He didn't like HR people. Nobody did, he assumed. And he *really* didn't like liberals either. And everybody knows that people who work in human resources can only be liberals. He'd always assumed they were hired, most likely, because they were either not caucasian, or not male. They were certainly not political conservatives. Luther himself was a white guy, and a conservative. This, he surmised, meant he was public enemy number one at the office, especially with HR. Yet he felt he was too good at his job to be fired for simply belonging to the wrong set of demographics. He *was* the top salesman, after all. He made the company's coffers ring like sleigh bells year round. When Luther Colgera talked on the phone it was a near-certainty that at some point Santa Claus would be coming to town for Blackstone & Harding. He had a smooth and calm radio-quality voice, and knew exactly what to say and how to close a deal. In the end, they all begged him to take their money. At least, that's how he envisioned his own prowess as a salesman. Luther also made a point of including his official company photo in his emails, but only on his *internal* emails. It was a nice passive aggressive way to remind everyone that yes, a white man contributed to the company having enough money to pay *them.* He believed he did more than just contribute, but ensured that they would all be paid. He saw himself as the chief rainmaker, and without him, there would be no income to alleviate the company budget, no stuffing for the turkey, no presents under the tree. The self delusion gave him a sense of *schadenfreude* knowing his role in the company rubbed the whole 'white patriarchy' thing in the faces of those whom he believed were his political enemies.

Luther leaned back in his chair and scrolled through the email. It was formatted like an ornate Christmas card. Borders of holly, barely legible calligraphy, and snowmen for bullet points. It was quite festive and must have taken hours to perfect. He was certain that some boot-licking admin, or possibly an intern, had been sanctioned to justify their existence by designing it over an unpaid weekend. But what was most interesting to Luther was that far below, at the bottom of the email, under the bold and colorful font, were the tiniest couple of lines about the mandatory nature of the party. The most important terms of a contract are always buried deep within the smallest text. Luther smirked. How many customers complained about never having read the tiny terms and conditions, which they often signed in their Luther-fed frenzy to become Blackstone & Harding clients? Oh, he understood the small print. That's where the real magic and authority lie. And in this case it was clear to him that the magic and authority said 'go to the office Christmas party or you'll be fired.' Though it didn't really say that verbatim, it was intimated, and Luther would not risk a pink slip. He was convinced that pink slips for white guys were always pre-prepared, on file and ready to distribute at the slightest infraction, by non-male supervisors. He would not give them the chance. He would be at the party. What the email did not state however, was *how* participatory one must be at the party, only that one must attend and stay for its entirety. So he scrolled back up and observed the snow-man bullet points. The whole affair would commence with a barbecue buffet.

"Nice" he murmured aloud. Then turning to Jeremy Cole, his fellow sales person the next desk over, "Looks like Texas Rib House is catering the Christmas party."

"I saw that! Just had lunch there yesterday with Watts. It's good stuff." Cole, like always, was over enthusiastic in his reply.

"Indeed." Luther was starting to feel a little less anxious about the party, seeing as how at least the food would be on point. He kept scrolling the bullet points. "Gift Exchange", "Party Games", "Board Games", and...

"Oh, *hell* no!" Luther exclaimed.

Cole looked at Luther, and Watts popped his head up from behind the cubicle facing the two.

"What's up? What's wrong, Luther?"

Luther sighed, not realizing his outburst had been external.

"Karaoke."

Cole looked at him with a puzzled expression, while Watts snickered.

"What? You don't do karaoke?" Cole hinted at mock offense.

"I'd say that's the best bit, Colgera!" Watts jabbed at him in his deep British accent.

Luther ignored their taunting. They were both a couple of high energy goofballs, stereotypical of most salesmen, who loved being the life of the party. While Jeremy Cole was your standard issue fraternity bro, Winston Watts was a bit of an anomaly. A dual citizen of the U.K. and the U.S., his voice resonated with the intelligent timbre of his homeland, while his behavior was more that of a used car salesman from Dayton. They both loved being the social butterflies of the office. They loved anything that would feed their extraverted proclivities. Luther Colgera was an introvert, and highly annoyed by the stereotypes they played into. Yes, an introverted salesman who dominated his outgoing loudmouthed colleagues. He envisioned them standing before the whole company singing karaoke and dancing together like a couple of buffoons; off-key, off color, and guzzling the attention.

As he returned his attention to the email, Luther despised every bullet-pointed activity except the food. A free lunch was a free lunch. Sure, you could serve it on paper plates with Santa faces printed on them and call it a Christmas dinner. To Luther it was no different than a picnic lunch paid for by the company in the middle of June.

"I'm just going for the food."

The two salesmen looked at each other, astonished that their senior salesman held the holiday in such low regard. Taking turns, they began to extol the benefits of Christmas and their lifelong love of its celebration. Luther held up his hand in warning. He picked up his phone and began to dial a phone number.

"I came to work to sell, not be sold. Let's get back to it."

Watts lowered himself back into his swivel chair behind his cubicle. Cole, whose face was red with annoyance at being admonished by a 'Christmas hater' turned back to his computer screen. Luther then proceeded to have a soft-spoken conversation over the phone, a fake conversation as no one was on the other end. It was simply a ploy to get Cole and Watts to back off, and break away from the Christmas small-talk. After a minute or two of this pageantry, he ended the faux sales call and headed out the door and down the hall to the restroom.

2

L uther skulked down the hallway muttering to himself.

"This is so stupid. I should be working from home, fulltime." He deplored being forced to commute to the office. His job and the tools he needed to do it were perfectly suited to working remotely. And he could do it without having to suffer the foolishness of his coworkers.

"I could be making more sales if I was doing this crap from home..." he approached the restroom door and flung it open while growling aloud, "...uninterru pted!"

The door flung inward but stopped halfway with a loud bang. Luther, who was moving at full steam plowed into the door smashing his face into it. For a moment, everything was a blur. The door was obviously blocked by something or someone, but Luther was still clearing the stars from his vision before it all became clear. Another voice, one from behind the door, exhaled in a half-growl, half-sigh.

"In a hurry?" the displeasure in the voice bordered on disgust.

Luther's vision cleared and he slipped through the half opened door into the restroom. An old man in a blue gray jumpsuit, stood with both hands on a rolling cart. The cart was full of chemical spray bottles, pristine rolls of paper hand towels and toilet paper. On the lower shelf of the cart was a grime smothered mop bucket half full of water, the color of mud and winter clouds with just one or two suds bobbing on the surface. The man was a perfect reflection of the cart, two manifestations of the same entity. His hair, which was to be found on the sides of his head just above his ears and above his lip, matched the color of the bucket's contents. The stubble that covered his cheeks and chin was as splotchy and mottled as the grime on the cart. His sunken shriveled eyes were blood shod in anger, though Luther could tell this was their default, the wrinkles gave it all away. Yet his blue gray jumpsuit was perfectly clean and kept, pristine like the untouched rolls of paper on the cart's top shelf. He held a mop in one hand, while the other was clutching the cart to keep it from toppling.

"Watch yer step," he barked. "I just did the floor and I don't need an accident on my shift."

Luther observed the floor was wet. And though the floor gave the appearance of being clean, it glistened with the muck that was in the bucket. Luther was less afraid of an injury from a fall, than he was getting his face close to the muck-water on the floor. He nodded at the janitor.

"Sorry about that. My mind was in another place and I wasn't paying attention." It seemed like a fitting apology, and for Luther's part it was heartfelt.

The janitor snickered and set to work replacing a paper towel roll. Luther caught a glimpse of the white oval patch above the man's left breast pocket. *Jenkins* it read. Luther made a note of the name in his mind right alongside the complaint of rudeness. This man had no interest at all in hiding his disgust for his job, the people who worked there, or anything other than the cleanness of his own clothes. The bathroom wasn't exactly clean, and it smelled. The cart, the bucket, and the man himself were all of a piece, dirty, ragged, and worn down with use. Only the man's clothes were crisp.

When Luther finished relieving himself he set to wash his hands. Jenkins was still fiddling with the paper towel dispenser, smacking it and muttering profanities. It was awkward pretending not to notice the janitor's fussiness and guile for every material object in the material universe. When Luther was ready to dry his hands, he realized that he'd have to ask the sour man for assistance, since the paper towel dispenser was still 'under maintenance'. He decided against it, wiped his hands on the sides of his pants just under the flaps of his sport coat and moved towards the still-blocked door. As he was squeezing his way out of the restroom, Jenkins suddenly noticed him again.

"You said 'uninterrupted'" he growled. Luther turned his head as the janitor set his beady black eyes on him. "When you came in here and pushed the door into my cart, you said 'uninterrupted. I'm sorry if my job is an *interruption* to you." The sarcasm was electrifying. The vitriol was not so much directed at Luther, he could tell, but at the human race in general.

"Oh sir!" Luther exclaimed. "You are not an interruption! In fact, I appreciate what you do quite a bit, keeping this place clean..." he glanced down at the muck sheen of the floors, "...and all."

The sarcasm was proportioned and subtle. *Service returned*, he snickered to himself.

"Then who's interrupting you?" Jenkins barked, challenged by what he believed to be a lie.

"Oh, I was thinking about..." he didn't want to be ratted out by the janitor for bad-mouthing his coworkers behind his back, "the Christmas party. It's mandatory. I'm a sales guy and time spent at a party is time spent not making money."

Something shifted in the janitor's eyes and the creases of his face. It was a knowing look with a hint of glee, fed by guile.

"The company Christmas party eh? Yeah well it's an interruption for me too. Who do you think has to clean up after y'all when the party's over? Oh sure everyone gets to go home at the end of the day but ole Jenkins. I gotta clean up y'all's mess. And for what? Christmas? Christmas ain't nothing but a pagan holiday anyway. Meant to keep cash registers ringing. Meant to give people one last chance to feel better about themselves before the reality of next year sets in. The government invented Christmas..."

The tirade was rich with conspiracy and lasted for a very awkward minute. Luther stood with one leg in the hallway, and one leg still straddling the restroom doorway. For some reason he could not pull away from the bitter old man. The claims Jenkins made were absurd, ludicrous, bombastic... yet Luther could not help but believe some of it. Christmas was a dismal time for him.

3

After work Luther hit a drive thru and purchased a cheeseburger, devouring it completely before he reached his apartment. From the time he crossed the threshold until falling asleep that night he was scouring the internet. He ran multiple searches for the 'pagan roots of Christmas', and the history of St. Nicholas. He read the Nativity story from the Bible then watched YouTube videos about the Babylonian imagery adopted by the Catholic church to promote the birth of Christ. He discovered that Christ wasn't even born on December 25th, nor did the three kings, who it turns out weren't even real kings, come to the manger that night in Bethlehem. Nothing about Christmas, if Luther was to believe all that he read online, could be trusted or believed. And Luther devoured all of it, wholesale. Anything that chipped away at the authenticity of the holiday, its meaning or value, was quickly memorized. Luther labored at his laptop, filling his mental arsenal with what he called 'facts' for dismembering the joy and meaning of Christmas others may try to impose on him. Feverishly he scrolled and searched and read. Article after article. Video after video. When his alarm went off the next morning, he awoke still fully dressed and on top of his blankets. The laptop was still open yet flipped over on the floor next to the bed. Luther jumped from his bed and blitzed through his morning routine. In the shower he regurgitated, out loud, many of the factoids he'd memorized the night before. He framed up his arguments, and prepared to do battle with anyone at the office who dared impose their Christmas spirit on him.

When he arrived at work, he marched to his desk with a 'just try me' air about him. His defense was in place. His guns were locked and loaded. But Cole and Watts were already on the phone working away. If Luther timed his own calls cleverly, he might stagger them in a way to always be on the phone when his colleagues were not, and not be busy when they were wrapped up in their own phone calls.

Each week, Luther had a one on one meeting with his direct supervisor, Torilo Kondo. He was a balding middle-aged Japanese American, who was shaped like the Buddha. His life was reports and emails, directives and hard conversations. It was all stress and high blood pressure with Kondo, without the inner calm and med-itation. Since their meeting was scheduled for that day, and it was the last one before the mandatory party, he resolved to gently broach the subject of attendance. *Who knows?* he thought. *Maybe Kondo will see reason and help me wiggle my way out of having to attend.* Toriko Kondo was what's known as a 'company man.' Intensely loyal to the company, he was also a brilliant sales manager. Depending on his mood or stress level, Mr. Kondo may be persuaded to exempt Luther. That's what he was hoping for. But when Luther entered his supervisor's office, There was no Buddha-like smile, and Kondo's sleeves were rolled up while his fingers were ravishing his keyboard. Luther cleared his throat to announce his presence.

"Ah! Colgera! I forgot the time. Sit down. We'll be quick with our meeting this week."

Crap, Luther thought. *Well, here goes nothing...*

Luther, with little time to spare, laid out his case from a practical standpoint.

"There's talk of a blizzard. The forecast is actually worse than it was yesterday when the company-wide email went out."

"And?"

"Well," Luther was careful not to sound disrespectful, "it seems a bit reckless, don't you think? All of us getting stuck here in a snowstorm? What if we lose power and nobody can get home?"

Kondo sighed and rubbed his bald head.

"I can't change the rules for everyone. I can't even change them for myself, Colgera. You have to be here."

He wasn't going to budge. In the past Kondo seemed reasonable enough with such requests, but this time...

"Mr. Carpenter has said there are no exceptions. Not this year. And unless he says otherwise, we'll not be letting people leave the party early like last time."

Luther felt shut down. There was nothing to do now but deal with it. Kondo looked at him from behind his desk. He leaned back in his chair and crossed his arms, his black brows furrowed toward Luther.

"Why is it you are not wanting to be a closer part of the team? What kind of message is that if my top salesman isn't at the mandatory party with his teammates?"

"It's not that. It's just..."

"Just what? You don't celebrate Christmas or something?"

Luther saw an angle.

"Actually, no. I don't."

Kondo grunted. "Wait. You claim to be a Christian, right?, So why are you so repulsed by the most Christian of all holidays?"

Luther began to regurgitate all he had committed to memory the night before. He laid out the pagan history of the holiday, the commercialization marketed with sentiment, the conspiracies.

Kondo rolled his narrow eyes half a dozen times while Luther gushed. He even removed his glasses to rub the irritation away.

"There are plenty of Christians and non-Christians here that celebrate Christmas and are required to attend, Colgera. You are no exception."

Luther stiffened in his chair and defiantly countered.

"So are you forcing me, against my convictions, to celebrate a religious holiday?" He at that point was treading on very dangerous ground with his director. Kondo himself was running out of patience.

Luther took another breath to calm himself, and as humbly as he could, recanted a line from Dickens, "you may keep your Christmas in your way, Mr. Kondo, but please allow me to keep it in mine."

"You can keep it however you want. But you'll do it *here* on the 20th alongside everyone else."

And that was the end of it.

"We're wasting time talking about it and you need to get back to work. So... anything else?" Kondo was tapping his chunky finger on the edge of his desk. Luther wanted to scream, but he knew where the red line was drawn with his supervisor and said nothing. Tight-lipped and beaten, he simply shook his head.

"Okay then," Kondo snickered to lighten the mood, "get out."

4

Luther's childhood home was a tiny two-bedroom house, more of a shack, in the poorest part of town. It was the better half of a duplex, which matched exactly the color and layout of all the other duplexes stamped into existence on Terry Street. There was no sidewalk on his street, and every driveway was plain gravel. There was no pavement beyond the concrete block that formed three gray steps that rose to the front door. And while paint was peeling on every house, for the landlord was negligent of the aesthetics, the Colgera's roof never once had leaked. Their windows were properly glazed and their tiny half of the duplex was easy and cheap to keep warm. Luther never saw the inside of any of the other houses, but assumed they all matched the tidiness and cleanliness of his own. His mother was meticulous about the condition of the shag carpet, especially in the living room, and the linoleum of the kitchen. And while the kitchen was always in a state of flux between pristine and cluttered from meal preparation, the bathroom, of which there was only one, was kept sparkling. The furniture was simple. Most of it was second hand and worn, but kept clean and clear. The walls were covered in cheap yet handsome frames of printed family photos, the majority of which documented the happy toddler years and young childhood of Luther's upbringing. Mom and Dad were in each photo as well, and most of the images had been carefully staged. Matching clothes, all of the same pallet with a background of either a city park in autumn, or the whitewashed entrance of their church during Easter. There were no candid moments hanging on Mrs. Colgera's wall.

Mr. Colgera, Luther's father, worked full time as a delivery driver for a local seafood company. He used his own vehicle, a rundown old passenger van with the seats unbolted and removed, for his work. The extra bench seats were leaned up against the back of the house next to the back door. They served as patio furniture during the summer, and lasted for years as they were made of waterproof vinyl. Mr. Colgera did his best to keep his van running smoothly, despite the hundreds of thousands of miles racked up in service to his employers, and for the sake of his own dignity he kept the interior clean of trash and dust. It wasn't enough to appease Mrs. Colgera, as Luther's father always came home smelling like cod and shellfish and the brink of spoiling. The hours of his labor never really fluctuated, affording him nights and weekends to fill with part time work. And the only viable service Luther's father had to offer their small town was delivery driving. So while during banker's hours he delivered smelly seafood to local restaurants and grocers, during the evenings he delivered pizza, and on weekends flowers for the local florist. There was no day of rest during the week, only the annual Easter, Fourth of July, Thanksgiving, and of course Christmas - four precious days a year to be home with his wife and son. And with the constant use of the old van, much of Mr. Colgera's hard-earned income went to the constant repair of something or other on the vehicle. The more he used it, the more expensive it was to maintain. So when one of those four off days rolled around, there was no money for vacations or outings. There was rarely money for new Easter clothes, and never a spare dollar for some fireworks. Thanksgiving was a meager feast at best, with a rotisserie chicken and instant mash potatoes; possibly pecan pie if a customer happened to tip Mr. Colgera during the season of giving. Christmas however never failed to yield at least a few presents for Luther under a very scrawny yet perfectly decorated tree.

At eighteen years old, Luther was perceptive enough to see the despair in his father's economic situation. Though for years Mr. Colgera had joyfully and contentedly made the best of his life's lot, he was determined that Luther should go to college, get a good job, and make a better life for himself.

"And then what?" Luther challenged his father.

"Well," Mr. Colgera countered, "maybe you'll get married or..."

Luther snickered at the thought.

"I'm never getting married. That's for sure."

When his mother asked him why, for she had dreamed, like every mother of adult children, for grand-kids, he shot back words that stung.

"Marriage is expensive. Why waste money on a wife if you're broke?"

Mr. Colgera cleared the frustration from his throat and took a drink of water. Luther's mom wrinkled her brow and shook her head at her son.

"Seriously though, Dad," Luther continued, "what good is getting married and having kids if you never have time for them?" The words weren't intended to hurt, but were put forth in earnest, yet in the challenging and cocky tone of adolescence. The question landed hard on the ears and hearts of the Colgera's, especially Mr. Colgera. The usual facade of cheerfulness melted from his countenance. His face reddened with feelings of both anger at his son's indolence, and shame for never making more of his family's situation.

"You won't be broke if you go to college and get a job. Jobs that require degrees pay a decent income, Luther. Then you can get married. Or not get married. It's your life so..."

"But Dad" Luther blindly continued to counter his father, "*you* went to college, right?

Mr. Colgera nodded.

"Well how did *that* work out for us all? How does a college degree help you *not* work three jobs?"

"I made some mistakes in my career path, sure..."

"Mistakes?" Luther's voice was getting louder and rising in pitch. The excitement was growing as unspoken anxieties, fueled by teenage hormones, began to spill out. The dam was cracking. "You had a business of your own and you had to sell it to pay off your debt. You moved us to this do-nothing town and got a do-nothing job and just... gave up!"

"That's enough, Luther" Luther's mother was ashamed at her son's disrespectful rant. But more than that, she could see something in her husband's eyes, a cold hard glint, and the glassiness that signals reason is packing its bags and making room for animalistic rage. "It's Christmas Eve. Let's just enjoy our dinner and not argue, okay?"

"No. It's okay Mandy. Let him talk" Mr. Colgera straightened his back and stared his son in the face with one elbow propped up on the table. "He's a grown man, now..."

The sarcastic challenge from Luther's father was not lost on his youth. It was less than subtle. Luther went on to give, quite tactlessly, his opinion of college's uselessness, marriage's conventional overestimation, and labor's meaninglessness. Of course, he'd never gone to college, been married, or had a job.

"Ha!" His father pounded the table with his fist. "Spoken like a true college student! A know-it-all with no life experience. An expert in the ways of the world, a philosopher, and I'm sure, a millionaire in the making. Do you know how many thousands of *kids* your age think they have it all figured out? Well let me tell you, *boy*. All of them. They all think that *they* are going to do things differently. *They* are going to change the world.

They understand how things *really* are, while their parents and everyone else, are idiots or lazy or misinformed or ignorant. Yeah, with that attitude you may as well just skip college, because you're already a know-it-all punk with no life experience."

"Fine. I'll just skip college, like I said."

"You're going to college Luther."

"But you just said..."

"What I was trying to say was that if you're going to be an arrogant know-it-all, you might as well have a piece of paper that proves it to your employer."

Luther was seething. He could tell his father was hurt, but never had sarcasm been a weapon used against him. He'd never seen his father quiver, with rage. Or was it regret? Luther could not tell. His mother left the table and busied herself with cleaning up the kitchen. It was too much for her to endure. Several silent minutes passed as Luther and his dad forced themselves to clean their plates. While Mr. Colgera was calming himself down and looking for ways to lighten the conversation, Luther was compiling angry accusations and snarky responses for the next round of arguing.

Mr. Colgera calmly and softly said, "I had a bad turn of luck in my business, but I'd never have met your mother or discovered what career to pursue if I hadn't gone to college, son. It's the next step in life for you. You can't skip it. Don't cheat yourself."

The gentle words found no 'room at the inn', and Luther continued in his full vigor.

"Yeah, I'd never want to skip the opportunity to be miserable, have no money, live in a crappy little house, and drive a crappy little van."

The sarcasm and vitriol in Luther's tone was too much for Mr. Colgera to handle.

"Watch your mouth, boy!" he snapped at his son. The air fizzed in an out of his nostrils.

"Hey son," Luther mocked his father, "you should go to school so you can one day come home each night smelling like rotting salmon and complain to your wife that your van is overheating again."

"Shut up, Luther!" The old man was fuming, on the brink of completely losing all control. Luther could smell the anger and the fear... or perhaps it was just the fish. The excitement of the moment, the threat of physical danger from his father, it was all so new; so thrilling, so stinky.

Luther continued the mimicry, "And one day when you have a little rug rat of your own, you can force him to go down the same smelly dead-end meaningless miserable path. He can be a loser. Just like his old man!" Luther was practically screaming. All restraint had been abandoned.

Mr. Colgera leapt from his chair, grabbed the edge of the dinner table and flipped it, dishes, glasses, food and all upside down. The noise was deafening. Little yippy dogs in the unit connected to theirs started barking. The police were called by neighbors on the other side of the wall and were on their way. Luther, shocked at his father's sudden explosion of strength and speed and jumped backwards out of his chair, which also flipped over. The fear that gripped him snuffed out his will to continue his snarky diatribe against his father. In fact, his will to confront his father at all had been completely squashed. He backed away from the raging hulking old man, who had in Luther's eyes grown several sizes and seemed to fill the entire room. Luther backed into the kitchen corner next to the sink. His father stood before him panting like a wild animal and gritting his teeth. Hurt and resolve pulsated from his bloodshot eyes as he glared at his son. Over the man's shoulder Luther saw the scrawny Christmas tree with its soft colored lights, silver tinsel, and ornaments all aglow yet strangely distant. The trauma of the moment seared the image into his memory. Luther's father noticed his son's eyes dart away briefly then back to him. There was a brief moment, only a second or two in which everything paused. There was some dark conversation happening behind the eyes of Luther's father that lasted only a moment. Luther said nothing, but only stood there helpless, hoping that his father would no longer see the threat of an eighteen year old man in his house, but instead see the quivering scared son who forgot his place. He was not prepared to hear the words come from his father's mouth, like a hammerblow to his mind. It shattered everything he believed, rightly or wrongly, about his dad.

"Get out!"

5

L uther skipped breakfast the morning of the office Christmas party. By the time noon rolled around his stomach was aching and grumbling. He was irritable, snippy, and if for nothing else excited to gorge himself on free barbecue. When the elevator doors opened he saw the feast all sprawled out before him. Two extra-long folding tables were placed end to end and were draped with plastic red tablecloths with giant white snowflakes printed on them. From end to end, a full sixteen feet, the table was covered with foil trays, buckets, and pans; each brimming with savory Southern meats and side dishes. There was a mound of pulled pork that filled its three by two foot pan, three inches deep. There was another pan half the size with smoked brisket. Buckets of mashed potatoes and bacon-cooked green beans. There were casseroles, mac n' cheese, and cakes of fluffy yellow cornbread. There were four different barbecue sauces, each spicier than the last, and various condiments in quantities needed to season the entire cornucopia, and then some.

Luther wasn't the first in line, but he immediately fantasized about shoving aside those that arrived ahead of him. Mostly, they were women. *Women should always go first,* he reminded himself, *and that includes the ones who should diet and have no business filling up on my barbecue.* He worried that there may not be any brisket left by the time he reached the middle of the table. Fortunately, the office staff lined up in two lines, one for each side of the table, yet no matter which side he chose to stand in, he was sure it would be the fatter and slower of the two. Luther felt a pang of sudden guilt. He was no doubt going to make a gluttonous run at the feast, yet now his colleagues knew his opinions about Christmas in general. It seemed almost hypocritical to eat Christmas' feast and not believe in its conventional charms and value. But he was mandated to be there like everyone else. When he reminded himself that it was his efforts as a salesman that made the feast possible his guilt was assuaged. Christmas feast or otherwise, the company could afford the bountiful dinner *because* he was good at his job. Luther stood tall as he waited to load up his plate.

When he reached the beginning edge of the table, the end with the stack of plastic plates, he took two of them so that the thickness would prevent his plate from collapsing from the sheer weight of his share of brisket and mac n' cheese. He focused on covering every visible area of his plate. Efficiency was paramount. It was a great art form, ensuring that only the right items made the cut and had the privilege of being devoured. They must all be perfectly arranged so that the juices or grease from one might not spoil or diminish the flavor of its neighbor, but enhance it instead. Thus, the Hawaiian roll must stand between the mac n' cheese and sauce-drenched meat, and not in the middle of the plate. It must be off to the side of the plate and only touching those two items, that way it would only absorb the spicy barbecue sauce or melted cheese and not the runoff from the green beans or grit from the mashed potatoes. The mashed potatoes themselves must form a perfectly shaped hill directly across from the roll, with a ladle-sized crater impressed in the top for the gravy. The gravy must not run. It must be contained in its divot until the Hawaiian roll is devoured. Then one may take that first bite of potatoes, breaking the dam and spilling the gravy down the sides of the lump and onto the bottom of the plate. And the green bean casserole... well, gross. That would not make it onto Luther's plate. Casseroles were for the lowlife masses who didn't care about flavor or their palette. Such people thought more of the fullness of their stomachs rather than the party of taste in their mouths.

Luther found himself holding up the line trying to hollow out the crater in his mound of mashed potatoes. The serving spoon chosen to facilitate the scooping of the potatoes was not deeply rounded enough and thus not suitable for cratering, much to Luther's irritation. While he didn't want to be a hypocrite by holding up the line, he wanted his plate to reflect the exquisite order it deserved. The sound of someone clearing their throat grabbed his attention. He looked up and directly across from him, awaiting his turn to self-seve the mashed potatoes, stood his supervisor.

"I don't want the gravy to spill all over plate," Luther sheepishly explained.

Mr. Kondo flashed an insincere grin without making eye contact, and was that a lip-smack? The body language could not be more clear. Luther needed to wrap up his engagement with the potatoes and move along. Slightly embarrassed, he handed the serving spoon to Kondo and, not wanting to give up on the work of art his plate was becoming, used his bare thumb to finish the work of hollowing out the crater. Then with a quick wipe of his thumb on his pants, he reached for the gravy.

By the time it was all said and done, Luther's plate was picture perfect, a presentation worthy of respect. Too good to simply dig into without first standing back, sighing with great satisfaction, and if one's smartphone was handy, sharing it with a thousand people who really don't care. He preferred to keep his social media posts strictly political, and strictly offensive. A photo of one's food did nothing to pick a good fight, and would attract no liberal trolls. Besides, he only posted from his laptop. He didn't even own a smartphone. He traded it in for a flip phone, intentionally, months earlier. Not having the digital distraction in his pocket helped him better focus on his work, and he made more sales calls than his comrades. It also gave his ego a twisted stroke when he had the opportunity to brag about his counter-cultural stance on technology.

In the event hall there were a dozen large round folding tables set up here and there around the stage. Each table hosted six to seven chairs and was draped with the same plastic red tablecloths with white snowflakes. However, the center of each table boasted a wide candle surrounded by a wreath of faux holly. Luther chose the table closest to the door in case he wanted to slip back to the food for seconds, and chose the seat that turned his back to the stage. He had no interest in what may happen on the stage and did not at any point want to make eye contact with anyone with a microphone. It was his way of saying, "I'm just here for the food."

Next to him sat Rose who worked in collections for the sales department. A newer hire, she was old enough to be Luther's mother. And though Luther had no interest in speaking with his mother during Christmas or any other part of the year, Rose was a great substitute for the moment. She was quiet and easy to talk to, or simply sit by without having to talk at all. The rest of the table filled up quickly with ladies from the bookkeeping department, and every chair was taken except the one to Luther's immediate left. Luther at first felt insulted, as if they were avoiding him, but he also enjoyed the extra space. But it was not to last. Oslo Parker walked into the event last of all, having arrived late to the party, and in his hands was the fullest plate Luther had ever seen. He of course made for the empty seat at Luther's left as it was closeby, and next to all his work mates. Oslo was the only male employee on staff in the bookkeeping department. He was a black man, quiet, extremely proficient at his job, and egregiously overweight. When he chose the seat next to Luther, it was assumed it was because of his largeness and disdain for walking unnecessary distances, and not that it was next to his coworkers. When Oslo settled into the chair, it squeaked and moaned from the weight. His plate landed with a distinct thud on the table, for there was no other way such a hefty plate could land. Luther's keen eye spied not two, but *three* plastic red plates stacked for reinforcement. *Impressive*, he thought. But that was the only thing about Oslo that could ever have impressed him. Though he'd met Oslo briefly when he first started at the company several months earlier, it was immediately obvious he had a reclusive disposition, and only showed enough social grace, if one could call it that, to not be voraciously rude. It could have just been a case of nerves on a first day in a new job among strange new people. But Luther took it as a slight, his dismal non-smiling way with people. He hadn't spoken to Oslo since, though he had seen him around the office on an almost daily basis. Luther noticed that he, like many of the other folks in Bookkeeping, was a smoker, was overweight, and though he didn't have a strip of dyed hair of either blue or purple like all the ladies in his department, he was black. These signals, along with Luther's perception of being cold-shouldered from any conversation with them, all validated his assumptions about their politics. As a salesman, he was an ardent capitalist. And that meant Republicanism was the remedy to the country's problems. Luther was not the kind of guy to go halfway on anything, so not only did he embrace right-wing politics as a conservative republican, he was vocal about it on social media, too. Just days earlier he had gotten into a virtual fist fight with some screeching whiny liberal girl. There were so many snarky memes and mean-spirited twists of rhetoric, that Luther, by the time he victoriously slapped shut his laptop, had forgotten what the argument was about or how it had begun. But he spoke his mind and shut down the young lady's argument with force and prejudice. That was all that counted. In truth, it was hard to leave his politics "at the door" when he arrived at work. It was a long-standing rule codified in the company's Code of Conduct. But more than that, avoiding political opining for the sake of fostering a team-like atmosphere was a deep-seeded part of the culture at Blackstone & Harding. Luther however saw the signs. The girl he had virtually publicly executed on social media also had a strip of blue dye in her jet black hair. That's what her profile picture revealed. Luther walked past the data entry cubicles on a daily basis for years. Seemingly against company policy, there were displays of leftist slogans, flags, and tchotchkes decorating the desks. Each cubicle was a shrine to some 'marginalized group', some socialist liberator, or progressive cause. This was their statement of politics; silent, colorful and loud - yet contained to the five by five realm each person had full autonomy to decorate. He wondered if putting up propaganda that signaled the virtues of his own right wing ideology would be equally acceptable. If his displays had equivalency in loudness, color and bombastic printed rhetoric, would they ask him, a white guy, to take it down? He assumed that would be the case. And so, he went about his day, keeping his mouth shut and feeling himself a victim, while accusing leftists of always acting like victims.

As the tables in the event hall finally filled, the company Director, Simon Blankenship, meekly ascended the dias and tested the microphone. The feedback loop that resulted was brief and left a ringing in the ears. After gauging an effective distance, Director Simon began the festivities.

"All right," he said with a soft smile. "Looks like we have sound, so let's get started."

The room hushed and all turned their attention to the director. Luther twisted round halfway, draping an elbow over the back of his chair, and slinging his left leg over his right. In doing so he accidentally rubbed his foot against Rose's leg. He apologized quickly repositioned himself, struggling to find a comfortable posture, when the Director began.

"Thank you all for being here today."

Did we have a choice? Luther smugly thought. The idea of being thanked for coerced attendance reminded him of being a child in his parents' home being thanked for doing the dishes, after being threatened with a spanking.

"I hope everyone has plenty to eat. Feel free to make second and third trips. I think we over ordered from Texas Rib House, so if anybody wants to box up some food when you leave, help yourself." Director Simon then cleared his throat then scanned the room. "I don't think we've ever had a turnout quite this good at our office Christmas party. But don't worry we've got a lot of fun things lined up for you guys to do over the next few hours. I know that Watts and Cole have something special that they've prepared. And we're going to do the gift exchange and games after we wave the white flag on trying to eat all this food. Watts brought a pile of board games, too, so if anyone gets 'board'", he used quotation fingers to punctuate his attempt at the pun, "feel free to grab an empty table. It could be a good way to get to know some people you don't normally interact with on a daily basis here at B&H. Also… and this wasn't in the bulletin… Mr. Blackstone (who was the owner of the company) has hired a caricature artist who should be arriving any minute. There's no charge if you want a picture drawn by the artist to take home with you. Well, that's pretty much it. Let me just add one more thing before I ask the blessing on the food. It's truly wonderful to work with such a wide group of talented, hardworking, kind people. You made me really proud this year and I hope that you each have a truly blessed and abundant Christmas."

There was a brief spattering of applause, then the director asked everyone to bow their heads. Luther didn't remember the words of the prayer, but noted that it was mainly about thanks for the food, and it being a blessing to our health and happiness, blah, blah, blah. When the word "amen" was finally spoken, the people all repeated and the energy in the room spiked. People began shoving brisket and green beans into their mouths as if Director Simon had ended his prayer with "Fight!" instead of "amen".

Luther calmly twisted around in his chair to face his plate. For a moment, he felt pity for all the food that was about to be ravished. He was going to battle. But like those legendary generals of bygone eras, he silently saluted his adversaries; the said adversaries being the mound of mashed potatoes and the heap of sauce-laden brisket. As he raised his fork up to his mouth, much like a fencer would raise his rapier at a duel's start, he couldn't help but notice how everyone else at the table bent way down, bringing their mouths close to their plates. It wouldn't have bothered him so much if the tops of their heads weren't streaked with different hues of purple, pink and blue. There was even a green strip of dyed hair. But every head at his table was lowered and every head, except Rose's next to him, had a streak of color. It reminded him of a dashboard full of gauges, with different colored needles all pointing downwards. *They're all running on empty*, he mused. *All empty of reason and common sense. All of them completely self-loathing, bitter and angry. Empty of happiness in their lives.* He then had another sensation come over him. He couldn't help but think of the irony of people so overweight being so entirely empty of happiness.

With scowling mouths full of greasy barbecue, there was no conversation at the table. He wasn't much for chit chat anyway, but it still seemed wrong somehow. The only person whom he felt comfortable talking to was Rose, who worked with him in his department. He scrambled to think of how to break the ice and begin a conversation that may set her, and any one else at the table at ease. There seemed to be a thick, almost palpable aura of discord hovering over the table. Everybody knew each other's politics, but dared not talk about it. Who knew? The next election could result in civil war, or violent unrest between conservatives and progressives. The tension was everywhere, Luther observed. *One wrong word and I might trigger one of these psycho liberals and ruin everyone's Christmas,* he thought. *Tempting.* But he decided against it, mainly because he really respected Director Blankenship, one of the only other white guys in the company (as far as Luther could tell), apart from him, Cole, and Watts. Simon Blankenship had been the one to build the culture of camaraderie and had insisted that politics be verboten at the office, at least as a conversation topic.

And of course, Luther didn't want to get fired.

He decided on a joke. Yes. A clean workplace-friendly joke would break the ice. He leaned over to his right and softly spoke to Rose. His tone, he thought, was just loud enough for only her to hear, without it being a creepy whisper.

"You know Rose," he began. "I once went to a vegan barbecue."

"How interesting! How did that go?" she politely replied. "You don't seem like the vegan type to me."

Luther snickered and replied, "Well, the vegan was overcooked. So..."

A blank look came over Rose's eyes as she struggled to realize it was a joke. When she did, she struggled for a few moments more trying to make sense of the punchline. Suddenly a loud barking sound erupted from Luther's left. Oslo, whose mouth was full of casserole, had overheard the joke. He immediately got it and laughed hysterically. His laugh was loud enough to grab the entire table's attention. Unable to stop, he bounced up and down, and pounded the table with his meaty fist. His boisterous chuckle was suddenly contagious, and others began to laugh not at the joke, but him. He was a spectacle to behold when laughing; his eyes twinkling, and shoulders bouncing up and down as if his massive belly was their trampoline. Whatever tension had existed in his mind a moment ago evaporated and he was in sudden full mirth. Luther realized in a moment that Oslo's way of breaking the ice was to laugh at a joke he wasn't intended to hear, and that opened the door for more humorous discourse. *That's surprisingly classy of him*, Luther thought. *Laughing at someone else's joke, even if it isn't funny, is a sign of good social etiquette.* That's what his mother had taught him when he was a young teen. Her advice, when he had applied it at school, actually opened the door to friendships. But he had noticed that the social graces that existed in the memory of his childhood seemed so sparse and forgotten by the adult world around him now. Luther saw an opening to make a better acquaintance of Oslo, and had another joke loaded and ready to share, this time with him directly. His chubby round cheeks were still inflated by his smile and his giggling was barely starting to subside.

Then he inhaled a piece of pulled pork, quite by accident.

The panic spread all over his face as it began to darken. His hands shot up to his throat, grasping and clutching in distress. The rest of the table sat stunned, unsure of what to do. People from other tables began to take notice.

"Are you okay"? Rose practically shouted.

"Oh my God! He's choking!" another declared

As people leapt from their chairs, some to assist Oslo, most to back away from the chaos, he toppled backwards and landed flat on the floor. He rolled from side to side, as Rose and Kondo, who had rushed over from his own table by Blankenship, tried to get Oslo upright. Unsure of how only one person might effectively apply the Heimlich maneuver on such a larger man, Luther grabbed his phone and flipped it open. But before he could dial 9-1-1, he glanced at the traumatic scene once more. Oslo lay struggling, his face almost black now. Rose knelt by his side trying to hoist him up but to no avail. Just then, Justine Truitt, the pathological animal lover and advocate, came flying in from across the room. The thud of her heavy military-style boots went before her.

"Stand back!" she yelled. And before anyone could figure out what was about to happen, Justine lifted her knee almost to her chin, then stomped her boot heel down on Oslo's belly. The popping sound was something unexpected. Even in the movies they don't exaggerate it enough. The sound of air gushing out behind a dislodged cork was the only thing Luther could liken it to. The wad of pulled pork shot straight up and slapped the foam tiles of dropped ceiling. It rained down in a dozen small shreds like confetti.

Oslo inhaled a massive gulp of air, then rolled over onto his side. Luther, stunned by it all, stood with his flip phone in his hand and his mouth agape. Rose sidled over to Luther and elbowed him, shattering his state of paralysis.

"That was some joke," she snickered.

"Yeah. It was one of my favorites until about thirty seconds ago. Thank God Justine knew what to do."

Luther stepped into the fray of women helping Oslo to his feet. He bent down and extended his hand to him.

"Are you okay?" he asked.

Oslo grabbed his offered hand and was slowly hoisted onto his chair.

"I'm fine, thanks."

"Didn't mean to hurt anybody with that joke. I mean, come on. It wasn't *that* funny," he smiled.

Oslo nodded and shrugged, then turned back to his plate and began feasting straightaway as if nothing had happened. As the tension in the room reset to non-emergency levels, people returned to their seats. Luther noticed that his legs were trembling a bit from the high moment of anxiety, the adrenaline had not yet run its course through his body. His few steps back to his own chair were deliberate and quaky. Before he could sit down, the thunder of military boots stormed up behind him.

"Was that a flip phone?"

Luther turned and nodded in the affirmative to Justine. She stood there, triumphant, the hero who saved a life, yet calm by force of will. *Strange*, Luther thought. *Suddenly she is chatty with me. I'd best be careful where this conversation goes.*

"Uh, yeah..." he slipped his phone from his pocket and flicked it open and closed. "I ditched my smartphone several months ago. Just trying to make some changes in my life. Shut down my social media profiles, too."

It wasn't a complete lie. The smartphone had been a horrific distraction to his work as a salesperson. Yet while he claimed to have shut down his social media profiles, in reality, he opened up a single anonymous profile with an alphanumeric username. While he trumpeted his detachment from smart tech and social media publicly, he was still just as addicted to the online rancor and discord as anyone else, much to his shame.

Justine locked her eyes on him. There would be no escaping a conversation, and he was certain that a political jab was coming. How could it not? Justine had every progressive Leftist symbol draping her cubicle. She often bragged, subtly, about her significant other's career as an obstetrician, whom she called her 'partner'. The implied boast being more around the same-sexism, than the prestigious career. Luther had seen Justine's social media profile a few nights earlier. He sometimes breezed by it to remember just how far the world has fallen from common sense and how sick people like to parade themselves around as normal. Little did she know that she was exhibit A in Luther's case against the politics of the Left. And she, like many progressives, loved to bait and trap people in their own words, he believed. Always looking for someone to cancel, and to be the hero that dislodges the bigotry of white men from the choking throat of society. *Here comes the boot,* he thought.

"I've heard," she continued, "that a lot of people have been doing that. What's it been like not having a smart-phone?"

It was a fair question. Luther hesitated as he scrambled for an angle, one that would not lead to a deeper conversation about politics, religion, or anything at all really. For a moment he felt as if he had left his body and was viewing the interaction from afar. Never did he think that he and Justine would end up having a conversation at a Christmas party, that she would give him the time of day, or that the topic would involve something they may actually have in common. For there was so little in common between them. At a loss for stratagem, he resigned himself to the truth, as it is usually less difficult to maintain.

"It's the best thing I've done for my mental and emotional health in years."

"Really!"

"Yep. My depression and anxiety, those two always seem to go hand in hand you see, have practically evaporated."

Justine looked away briefly, a flit of the eyes as something like a nerve was struck, or perhaps she was like Luther searching for words and also landed on the simple truth.

"That's amazing actually. I've been wanting to do something like that too. I have friends that would kill me for it, though."

Luther understood completely. The fear of abandoning the digital tribes of political comrades was a real thing. Though experience had better informed him that there was less to fear than imagined.

"I felt the same way, Justine. You know what the biggest unforeseen benefit of all was when I got of 'social'? Nobody reached out to me to ask why. Nobody emailed me or called me wondering what happened to me. It seemed like nobody, and I mean this in the best way possible, really cared. In fact, when it comes up in conversations, I get the same response."

"What's that?" Justine was leaning in, intense for the answer; a genuine and vulnerable curiosity.

"They respond just as you did. They all say something like, 'I've been wanting to do that too,' or 'Congrats,' or 'You give me hope.'" Luther chuckled. "They never do it though. But at least they know that there is one person who was crazy enough to try it, and that it can be done."

"I don't think it's that crazy at all," she replied. "I get so wrapped up in knots watching people argue about politics, then I join in and... it makes me feel dirty and angry. It's no wonder people are so depressed all the time."

Luther held his breath. He couldn't tell if this was part of the trap or if Justine was being serious. The logical part of his brain was saying that it had to be a set up. But his gut feeling, something he as a salesperson had learned to listen to, told him that she was truly sincere. Luther grabbed his plate from the table, and his red plastic cup of sweet tea.

"Where are you sitting?" he asked.

"Oh, I'm done eating. The excitement of Oslo choking kind of robbed me of my appetite."

Luther felt a twinge of rejection, and was a bit disappointed that the conversation couldn't continue. Something seemed foreign and splendid about the whole interaction, but it could not go on. The Fates had spoken.

Justine was about to say something else, a continuation of a thought, but as she inhaled, Blankenship's voice boomed from the event hall's speakers.

"Okay everyone! Oslo is fine, for which we're all grateful. Thank you Justine for your quick thinking. Your method was a bit more violent than what I'd typically expect. But effective. Oslo lives and the party is still rolling along. So thank you."

At that moment, the room erupted with applause for both Oslo, whose life was spared, and Justine who so brazenly saved it. With all eyes on Justine, they were also on Luther, who stood next to her. While he, an ardent conservative white guy, was caught red-handed associating with whom he assumed was his political adversary, he could not help but feel a bit of pride in knowing her better. He flopped his plate and cup back on the table to free up his own hands for applauding her.

"Refresh your drinks if you want," Director Blankenship continued, "but set your plates aside and join us for a gift exchange."

6

Luther was the only person to go back for a second helping. Everyone else had left their plates at their tables, along with their cups, and gathered in a circle. It was a huge circle of almost fifty folding chairs. Cole and Watts had them quickly arranged within only two minutes. When the chairs were in place, two giant plastic garbage bags were retrieved from the stage. Each bag was stuffed with small packages wrapped in Christmas themed wrapping paper. No two gifts were the same shape, and the quality and skill of the wrapping varied widely, Luther noted. He himself observed from afar, as he did not want to participate in the gift exchange. He never did in the past, at previous Christmas parties, nor did he want to spend the time and money - off the clock - finding a gift that fit the criteria for the game. It was silly. That is what he didn't like about it. And it was such a waste of time. He did not care much for the giving of gifts, nor did he expect to receive any at Christmas. He desired only that which he had earned, with maybe a little bonus on top every now and then if he hit his quota. But Christmas gifts for fellow strangers in the office? He'd rather not. *Why should I*, he thought, *spend time looking for a gift that twisted and ungrateful leftists may like?* He couldn't imagine what kinds of things they would appreciate as a gift anyways, apart from bullhorns for protesting, nose piercings, and fake ballots. The thought alone of shopping and browsing for a suitable gift, trying to solve that puzzle, gave him a shot of trite anxiety. Besides, Luther was one to abhor the crowds during the holiday season. Stores filled elbow to elbow with people who had no idea they were being socially engineered to hyper consume, in most cases indebting themselves for crap they didn't need, nor would anyone really care for. For practically every gift purchased, Luther believed, it would be forgotten or tossed aside long before the debt had been paid off by the gifter. Yes, there was every reason to opt out of the gifting festivities.

He slipped out of the room and back into the hallway where the food was set up. He had total access to the entire buffet, and there was everything sprawled out before him once again. There was plenty of food left over for the entire office to make a second, and possibly third pass - with the exception of his beloved brisket. In the first round of feasting every pinch of that delicious smoked flesh had been claimed and devoured. Luther was disappointed as it was the item he loved most, but he was willing to settle for pulled pork as a substitute. Fortunately the spicy barbecue sauce still remained in abundance, and mounds of mac n' cheese still simmered over the Sterno burners. Before he began scooping more helpings of "roast beast" and sides, laughter broke out in the event hall. The gift exchange was underway. Luther opted out, of course. He had no choice even if he changed his mind at the last minute. He never bothered to draw a name for whom he'd then go shop for, with the goal of flaunting his gift-giving prowess before the office. And that thought applied to the entirety of what made up Christmas; it's traditions and formalities, it's decorations and colors. There was no point in learning the customs and expectations of a holiday one doesn't celebrate. In fact, the point was to *not* learn any of it. Luther's standoffishness was also his stand-out-ish-ness. He saw no difference between the two.

His plate reasonably refreshed, he sauntered over to the table with drinks and desserts. A moment of conflict arose in his mind as he realized that his stomach was only big enough for one more plate which in that moment did not leave much room on it for any of the sweets. Pecan pie and shortbread cookies had caught his eye, yet the real estate on his plate didn't allow for it, unless he returned some pulled pork or mac n' cheese. But that would involve scooping food from his dirty plate and putting it back into the serving pans, a slight infraction of healthcode rules no doubt. Also, it was just bad manners. He could simply throw the extra food away to make room for the pie and cookies, but tossing it in the garbage was a complete waste of delicious barbecue. His mother would have soundly punished him as a child if he threw uneaten food in the trash. He quickly pushed the thought of his mother out of his mind and made his decision. He peeked into the event hall just to make sure there was no chance of anyone walking his way. Nobody was looking. They would never know. He slipped back into the hallway, just out of sight of everyone playing the gift game, and tossed a couple of tongs-worth of pulled pork back into the pan from his plate. With a quick step to the side he stood before the mac 'n cheese and scooped two heaping spoonfuls back into the serving tray from whence it came. His plate then looked ready. Lots of space stared back at him, just enough to pile on the pie and shortbread.

"I saw that," growled Jenkins. He had emerged out of nowhere, seemingly, cart and all. Luther jumped at the sound of his voice. Mostly this was from surprise, though the sound of Jenkins' voice was unpleasant enough on any occasion to make one's skin crawl.

Luther played the fool.

"Saw what?"

"Saw ya take dirty food of yer dirty plate and plop it back into the pan. You tryin' to get everyone sick? Stupid and reckless thing to do during flu season. And Covid is going around again, ya know, not that it's anything other than a severe cold. I had Covid four times already and it never once slowed me down. It was all a ruse..."

Jenkins went on like a music box, wound up tight and suddenly let loose. Once he started talking he locked onto the rails of political conspiracy. His monologues seemed endless. Luther, at first worried Jenkins would rat him out about the food, simply nodded as Jenkins talked. The silent affirmations kept the old janitor rambling. After a few minutes of nodding at the janitor's bigoted ranting Luther sidled over to the sweet tea. He refilled his cup while seemingly still paying attention to the details of Jenkins' discourse.

I'll slip away when he's not looking, Luther thought to himself. Jenkins set to work removing a full trash bag from the large can next to the event hall door, and replacing it with another from his cart. But he didn't take a breath. he stood between Luther and the glowing festivities, his mouth a nonstop spigot of political bile. Luther was wondering if there was a bottom to Jenkins' barrel of opinions, or if he could go on forever. He had no interest in finding out, though some of what Jenkins said made some kind of sick sense. Just then a burst of laughter from four dozen people caught Jenkins' attention. He slowly turned his withered wrinkled old head towards the event hall, but only for a moment. Luther was dismayed when Jenkins began a fresh rant about Christmas.

"Suckers," he began. "They don't even know they're celebrating the birth of Nimrod."

Luther's ears twitched. He remembered something about that name when he was gathering anti-Christmas propaganda online.

"Yeah. I heard that December twenty-fifth was actually the birth of Nimrod and not Jesus."

"Babylonian worship. That's what Christmas is. What's it's *always* been," the old janitor snarled. "It's a psy-op to distract Christians into pagan idol worship."

Luther smiled, half in agreement and half in amusement. *Jenkins may prove to be a useful resource,* he thought. This was just the kind of intellectual ammo Luther needed to keep people from forcing the holiday down his throat.

"Yeah, wasn't Jesus born in like, March or something?"

Jenkins snickered as he tossed the full bag of trash into a rolling bin. The bin had been dragged along behind the mop cart.

"Nope. It's even weirder than that," he turned and squinted his beady black eyes. His nostrils flared and a twisted grimace formed around his stubbled cheeks.

"Guess again," he ordered.

Luther thought about all the dates on the calendar, all the important recent events that had half-morphed into national days of recognition. He knew that this old curmudgeon would somehow connect the paganism of Christmas to the government. That is, after all, what makes a truly great conspiracy.

Luther raised one eyebrow above his black-rimmed glasses, "September eleventh?"

"Yep," Jenkins immediately affirmed. In fact his response was so quick that Luther felt a bit robbed of his wild guess being right. "Nine eleven. Perfect, ain't it? No one's gonna be thinking about Jesus on that gloomy day, am I right?"

"It makes sense, I guess."

"You guess?" Jenkins practically spat the words. "Look, kid. Where there's smoke, there's fire. Next time nine-eleven rolls around, I dare you to tell someone that it's Jesus' actual birthday. You'll be skinned alive for being a conspiracy theorist." The last two words were punctuated by a quotation gesture, and Luther noticed the unlit cigarette between Jenkins' fingers.

"I'm going out for a smoke," he grunted. "You can join me if you want…"

Though it was tempting, Luther declined the invitation.

"I can't leave the party. Blankenship's orders. In fact if I don't get back in there, I could get an earload from my boss."

Jenkins scowled and waved his hand as if swatting Luther away like a fly. There was a very "you're dead to me" vibe about it. The janitor's dismal company was mentally and emotionally draining. The tender moment with Justine only a few short minutes ago had vanished.

He was in a funk about Christmas again.

Jenkins slithered off pushing his mop cart, and pulling the rolling trash can behind him at the same time. Luther walked back into the event hall and sat down at a table not too far from the wide windows looking into the parking lot. The snow was falling in massive flakes, and sticking just a bit longer than it took to melt from the asphalt. The angle of the falling flakes indicated that the wind had picked up quite a bit since he arrived that morning. The dingy orange street light struck the falling snow in such a way to make it mesmerizing to watch. Luther devoured his pie with his feet up on the window sill and his back to the circle chairs filled with gift-exchangers.

I'm here because I have to be, he told himself. *I'm no pagan, but I have to do what's necessary, just enough to keep this job.*

The gift exchange eventually devolved into the general white noise of random conversations. The games over, people were gobbling up the unplanned time opening their gifts and chit-chatting about Christmas plans. Luther couldn't care less and kept to himself by the window. He monitored the falling snow, half-heartedly wishing it would stick. While he didn't want to be snowed in and stranded at the office, it would be a nice thing to see the leadership of the company think twice about making future parties mandatory. A mandatory party at the jeopardizing of people's safety? *I tried to warn them,* he gleefully thought. *That'll teach them to not force people into joining their stupid little reindeer games.*

"Alright guys. Me and Watts have something special for you!" Cole's voice boomed, a bit suddenly and certainly a bit too loud. He had grabbed a microphone that was plugged into what Luther rightly feared was a portable karaoke speaker.

"Watts, get up here. Watts?" Cole scanned the room and the joyful crowd looked in all directions for the old salesman.

"Hey Luther!" Cole barked. "Will you go check the men's room and tell Watts we're waiting on him?"

Since he was closest to the door, Cole singled him out for the errand and did so publicly. Luther, being the top salesman felt a jab in his pride - a junior sales person giving *him* an order in front of the entire office! Oh yes, it rubbed him the wrong way. Cole was younger than Luther, too. The whole thing felt very condescending. Luther slowly got to his feet and nodded, but did not smile. With the slowest movements possible he lumbered towards the doorway to go fetch the older Watts. Stewing in his mind was a growing resentment for the overly outgoing and presumptuous Cole. But before he could concoct a subtle plot to jab back at him Luther heard banging on the glass double doors in the lobby. The banging was hard and rattled the glass, as if someone were angry. And someone was angry indeed. It was Watts, standing out in the snow with no coat on, one hand tucked under his armpit and the other balled up in a fist pounding on the glass doors of the building. Steam escaped his blueing face, which contorted with pain and irritation.

"Hey Luther! Lemme in! Doors locked!"

Luther calmly pressed the bar of the door and it swung outward. A blast of wind carried the bone-chilling air, along with a healthy billow of unwanted snow into the lobby. In came Watts like a frozen storm cloud, stamping the snow from his feet and searching the room with a feverish glare.

"Where is he?"

"Where's who?"

"That janitor."

"Jenkins?" Luther asked. "Haven't seen him for a while, but Cole was looking for you..."

"Cole can wait. I'm going to give that janitor a piece of my mind first." Watts trembled with anger and looked resolved to endure injury by either an altercation or heart attack. His blood pressure was skyrocketing. "He locked me out of the building on purpose. Could've frozen to death if you hadn't come along. that scoundrel!"

Watts was the only human being alive still using the word 'scoundrel'. It rolled smoothly off his tongue, but sounded strange reverberating in a stale, tope infested corporate office building. Luther suddenly felt a stronger affinity for the old Brit. He was a splash of color in a forcefully grey moment.

"Consider the rescue my Christmas gift to you, Watts. You're welcome," Luther quipped. But his jest was not received. Watts was burning too hot with annoyance."So what exactly happened, Watts?"

They walked back to the event hall together while the old salesman recounted the incident.

"After the gift exchange I needed to use the loo so I excused myself. When I strolled through the lobby I noticed that the janitor's cart was propping open the front doors and letting the cold air in. When I investigated further I see the man himself, if you want to even call him a man, more of a twisted mongoose, and he was standing just outside the doors trying to light a cigarette but his lighter wasn't working. So I thought I'd give him a light and join him for a smoke. Nobody ever really talks to him from what I'd always observed, and it's no wonder why now, but he's here having to deal with our

Christmas party mess, so... It just seemed like a nice thing to do, being Christmas and all."

"No good deed goes unpunished, Watts." Luther replied, unsure of what else to say, yet still irritated at his own cliche.

"Too right, Luther! I give him a light and stand out there making chit-chat with him while I have my cigarette. Not much for cheery conversation, I'll tell you. He's a sour old tosser. Did you know that? Have you ever spoken to him?"

Luther nodded. "I ran into him a time or two."

"Well now, I said 'Happy Christmas' to him when he finished his cigarette, and he waved his hand at me like, like..."

"Like you were a fly and you were annoying him?"

"Exactly. As if he was saying 'you're dead to me.'" Watts was deeply offended by the lack of courtesy, even after two decades of desensitization to American rudeness. The janitor's slight rattled his English bones. He shook his head as he continued. "He went back inside and pulled the doors shut behind him. I hear the click of the lock, so I rapped on the glass to get his attention, hoping he'd not accidentally lock me out in the cold. Well, he here's my tapping on the glass, but he turns to me and mouths the words *Merry* Christmas', then grabbed his cart and started rolling away down the hall. I pulled on the doors, which he'd locked on purpose I see that clearly now, and started to panic. So I begin pounding on the doors to get his attention. He completely ignored me and walked away. The tosser!"

Luther affirmed Watts' right to get even with Jenkins, even on Christmas. But Watts had cooled down a bit by the time they got back to the event hall and rejoined the party. He ascended the stage and grabbed the mic from Cole, who was having a bit too much fun with an impromptu game of trivia with the crowd of coworkers.

"Sorry folks," Watts explained. "Stepped outside for smoke and got locked out of the building! Took a minute to get back in but here we are, very awake and very ready to entertain you."

Cole flicked a switch on the karaoke machine, which suddenly activated the echo effect in their microphone. Seconds later a backing track of Bing Crosby's White Christmas began to play. Some stood with their red plastic cups in their hands and listened, while others found a chair and took a load off. Luther was the only one who didn't sing along. He was tempted to. He knew the words of course. Everybody knew them. But knowing the words and choosing not to sing them was the point of his silent protest against Christmas, and having to celebrate it by mandate. As the crowd boisterously followed the swooning voices of Cole and Watts, Luther thought about Jenkins' act of mean-spirited pettiness towards Watts. It was indeed a very jerk move. Watts was a borderline elderly man and getting locked out in a snowstorm could have had some serious consequences. *It's not exactly attempted murder or anything,* he thought. *But Watts should know his audience before ramming Christmas down other's throats.* Thoughts like these intensified as Cole and Watts became more and more off-key and off-tempo. By the time the song was over, the whole room was rolling with laughter, and Luther was seriously considering finding Jenkins and asking him to flick the breaker that controlled the power to the event hall. He suspected the old janitor would more than happy to oblige if he asked, but Luther refrained himself.

The next song began, Jingle Bell Rock. Rose and Justine bounced out of their chairs in surprise and leapt onto the stage. Where the off-key wonder duo of Watts and Cole had previously MC'd, now there was a quartet. The energy in the room elevated slightly, and people cheered. The tempo of the song was apparently perfect for kicking one leg outward then the other, like the Rockettes. The chorus line boasted Watts' high-end loafers, Cole's and Rose's sneakers, and Justine's combat boots flicking out to one side and then another. This, the two salesmen and and two ladies did for the entire song, while the rest of the crowd stood to their feet and swayed back and forth, in impressive synchronization. The laughter was contagious. The joy was overwhelming. Luther' thoughts of having the power cut no longer lingered. His brain had no vacancy for petty acts of anti-Christmas terrorism. He wasn't running to join the chorus line on stage, of course. Nor did he sway with the crowd of reveling coworkers. But he was certainly not going to ruin their fun. He remained in the back of the room near the windows, observing their swaying backs, and wondered what they looked like from the front, from the raised stage. Surely it was even more entertaining.

Suddenly every phone in the room lit up. A new chorus of harsh screeching digital warbles and beeps distorted Jingle Bell Rock. Cole, in the throws of Christmas euphoria turned the music volume up higher and signaled to the crowd to sing louder and ignore the digital interruption. This was somewhat effective, but a few people nervously read the emergency message, texted to them by the National Weather Advisory.

Luther grabbed his primitive flip phone and read the same: BLIZZARD CONDITIONS EMINENT. ROAD CLOSURES UNDERWAY. REMAIN INSIDE. SEEK SHELTER. CLOSURES EFFECTIVE UNTIL 8AM TOMORROW MORNING. Luther looked outside once again, the snow had definitely picked up. It billowed across the parking lot in thick sheets. The lights in the parking lot were blotted out and the sound of hard wind pelted the glass of the windows. The room grew silent as each person read the public service announcement. The mood quickly darkened in the event hall, as all, including Luther, realized that they were stuck at the office, not by mandate, but by force of nature.

7

L ooks like I arrived just in time. The janitor let me in."

Luther turned at the sound of the unfamiliar voice. A very lovely woman, short but stunning, stood in the doorway of the event hall. Her black hair was short cut to chin length. A smart beret the color of holly berries matched the thick scarf wrapped two times around her neck. Tucked under the arm of her peacoat, was a collapsible wooden easel. Her other arm held a soft leather briefcase. It was packed to the brim with canvases and blank papers, and it rattled with the sound of loose pencils as she walked, or rather bounced, across the room to greet Director Blankenship. Even from across the room Luther could not help but notice the brightness of her blue eyes. He wondered how long she had to stand out in the cold, knocking on the glass, before Jenkins let her in. The thought of Jenkins dragging that out for his own sick pleasure maddened him.

An elbow nudged him from his trance.

"That's the caricature artist Simon was talking about," Cole grinned. "Looks like there is something about this party you may enjoy, Mr. Scrooge."

Luther snickered but did not reply. Cole would have been correct about something at the party that Luther could enjoy. However, the news of the blizzard was too dismal an announcement to be brightened simply by the sight of a beautiful woman.

The artist chatted quietly with director Blankenship for only a few moments. Then she fired off a few texts and began setting up her easel.

"Who would like to go first?" she softly offered to everybody nearby. People still seemed phased from the news of being trapped in the building by the blizzard. They looked at each other in silence. At a time like this how could anyone enjoy another activity? Luther snickered and turned away. Nothing had dampened his holiday cheer because he had none to begin with. His excuse for being extra broody and moody was simply being held hostage by the weather. And even that didn't fully annoy him. In fact, there was a bit of a triumphant smirk on his face. He had warned Kondo about the weather. They should have listened to him. Of course, nobody ever wanted to listen to the pessimist. Even if they knew he was right about the weather, heeding his warning would have meant canceling or rescheduling the party. That would have been too much of a blow to corporate ego for them to ever take such advice from a lowly salesperson. And now their corporate pride was paying a steep price. Yes, Luther was in fact feeling pretty good about himself, though he was trapped. Surely now people would stop trying to ram the Christmas cheer down his throat.

"Well, I've got nothing better to do and nowhere to be so," Rose said. She smiled with head held high and waltzed over to the artist and took a chair.

Director Blankenship grabbed the microphone and commended Rose for making the best of the situation. Others began to concede to their fate, slowly. One by one they gave up being shocked about the news of the blizzard and began to line up behind the chair that Rose had taken before the artist. Within a few minutes the line was packed with people chatting and laughing together, lost in the moment. Cole and Watts returned to their karaoke machine and continued to sing, this time with the volume at about half the previous level. They serenaded the group with more songs; traditional carols like O Come All Ye Faithful and Angels We Have Heard On High. To Luther's surprise, Justine and the other data entry liberals were singing along. Their voices rang out more vibrantly than the streaks of color in their hair. It somehow didn't seem right to him. How could these people who were so politically extreme and seemingly godless join in carols about Jesus and Bethlehem? Luther felt flustered, almost offended that they would sing about *his* god, *his* religion, and *his* holiday. Then he reminded himself that though he claimed to be a Christian, Christmas wasn't really *his* holiday, but that was by his own choice. Still, it was still his prerogative to celebrate or not celebrate since it was after all his religion.

"Having a good time, Luther?" Oslo asked him. He had waddled over to a nearby folding chair and sat down. He was too apprehensive, due to his size, of standing in a line for who knows how long.

Luther slunk into a chair next to him and crossed his leg.

"Yeah. I guess."

"Tell your face then," Oslo countered. "You look like you're about to kill someone."

He had been unaware that his thoughts were manifesting in his countenance.

"I'm just pissed that we're stuck here all night. I tried to warn Kondo..."

"What do you care?" he asked. "I thought you were single. You don't have a wife or kids waiting on you like most everybody here. Most of our families are freaking out right now." Oslo took a long slow drink of yet another cup of overly sweet tea. "But maybe I'm just making assumptions about you. You got any family?"

"No," Luther lied. He squirmed slightly in his chair when the thought of his mom rolled through his head. There was a shard of guilt, irritating his heart as he thought about her sitting at home by a Christmas tree decked out in ornaments from his childhood. Sitting there alone, wondering where her son was, or if he was even alive. His mind raced back to his desk upstairs, to all the unopened letters his mom had mailed to him at the office, to the shredder they all found their way to, and to the bottle of bourbon hidden in his file drawer. It puzzled him how his mom had found out where he worked. He'd tried hard to keep his life private, from the eyes of his parents whom he'd hidden from out of spite. But his mom sleuthed out a way to contact him, and a few years earlier the letters started appearing in the company post box. He never answered them. He never opened and read them. They went straight into the shredder.

"It's just me."

"Don't you ever keep up with distant family though, like through Facebook or social media?"

"I don't do social media," he lied again. "I deleted my accounts a couple years ago."

Oslo's eyebrow went up slightly. "Oh really? Wow. That sounds like a lonely way to live. No family. No friends online."

"I get out some. I mean I do have friends. Real ones. Not that fake online stuff."

"Sure," Oslo smiled and drained his cup and changed the subject. "You gonna get your portrait drawn by the artist?"

"Nah. I don't really go for that sort of thing."

"Too bad. I'd love to but my knees... I can't stand in line that long. Besides," Oslo chuckled and slapped his own belly, "she'd probably have to turn the canvas sideways."

Luther didn't know what to say. He appreciated the self-deprecating humor but couldn't empathize with being overweight. He was careful to keep in shape. He looked good in a sport coat, and everybody knows that the C-suite doesn't invite obesity to sit at the board room table. But it does invite being a white guy if said white guy played his cards right. The first step towards a promotion was to overperform in his role. That was easy. The next step is to look the part of a leader. He'd heard some motivational coach, once upon a time, say that one should always dress for the job that one wants. One should dress as sharp as the CEO, or the owner of the company, but not better. Luther had never seen the CEO or owners of the company before, Messrs. Blackstone and Harding. In fact, the highest ranking person he'd ever met at H&B was Director Simon Blankenship. So, Luther closely observed the dress and mannerisms of the director, and modeled as closely as he could his own personal presentation and appearance. It was the classic 'old money' look - navy sport coat, khaki pants, pinstripe shirt, no tie. Well, not on casual Friday anyway. Fridays called for the entire ensemble sans neck tie. But the brown loafers were his daily footwear of choice seven days a week, yes even in shorts on sunny weekends. This was his uniform, and though he was still relatively young, the old money look made him stand out as a future leader within the company, or so he assumed. How far he had come from his upbringing. His father used to come home smelling like day-old seafood, dressed in a blue jumpsuit. He was a college educated man doomed to blue collar work, a man who'd failed to make himself something and traded in his dignity for a paycheck. Luther was determined to do differently, to do immeasurably better. He would *succeed*. He would achieve corporate knighthood, become one of the ruling class. He would show his peasant father that the son was the greater man. And when he'd attained his seat at the board room table of Blackstone & Harding, he would *then* reconnect with his parents and return home with something to rub in his father's face.

Rose returned to the table where Luther and Oslo sat observing the party. She sat down and with a big smile on her face laid her caricature sketch on the table.

"She did such a great job! Check it out."

Oslo leaned over while Rose pointed out the exaggerations of all her best, and worst, features in the drawing. The image was of her dancing to the tune of Christmas music, with a couple of quickly sketched goofballs in the background singing karaoke. Rose herself was wearing a hula skirt and sporting what looked like a lei made of a string of Christmas tree lights, the type with the oversized bulbs. In her hair was a piece of mistletoe instead of an hibiscus. Her eyes were squinted shut and her cartoonish smile was the broadest feature, drawing the eye inward. Joy was the theme of her caricature.

"Humph. Nice," Luther murmured.

"You should do it, Luther. She's really sweet to talk to and you'll have something to take home with you."

"I'll pass, thanks."

Rose scowled and stomped her foot. His refusal to be merry was starting to show, as was the irritation it caused in others.

"Don't be such a Scrooge. You didn't do the gift exchange with us, and you won't do karaoke. All you've done is eat more than your share of brisket and sit in a corner."

"So?"

"So, when it's all over you won't have anything to take with you. And you're missing all the fun."

Luther rolled his eyes, "you call getting snowed in at the office fun?"

"No," she countered, her voice growing sharp like a scolding mother's. "But I do call getting snowed in with your friends during a Christmas party fun."

Luther clammed up. His anger was starting to rise. Christmas was being rammed down his throat. He dug his heels in and sank deeper into his smug defensive opinion of it all. Out of the corner of his eye he noticed Jenkins roll quietly into the event hall. He pushed an empty rolling trash can over to a corner and swapped it for a full container. The grimace on his face made it obvious that he was trying to ignore the presence of joyful merry-makers, and at the same time hating their reason for being there. He was, after all, snowed in with them - and in his broken thinking, *because* of them.

"You all are a bunch of suckers!" Luther barked. "You are celebrating the birth of Nimrod and don't even re-alize it, Rose." The insanity gushed out his mouth. They all just stared at him as he continued to regurgitate the bitter words he'd heard not two hours earlier.

"Babylonian worship. That's what Christmas is. What's it's *always* been," he snarled. "It's all a psy-op..."

Rose's face was visibly angry. And Oslo's face dropped and he leaned back in his chair and crossed his thick arms in disgust. Luther could tell that his moment of indiscretion had caused him to cross a line and cause offense in his coworkers. Not that they were friends to begin with, but his words had certainly more clearly defined his attitude towards their merry-making, and his opinion of them. This did not deter him. As he opened his mouth to double down on his diatribe, Cole appeared at Luther's elbow, and just behind him, the caricature artist.

"Hey guys," Cole's voice brimmed with enthusiasm. "I asked Ms. Yilmaz here for a special Christmas favor. Oslo, I know you don't like standing in line because of your knees, so we thought we'd come to you and have your picture drawn!"

Oslo's attention was wrenched from Luther's foul assault on Christmas, and his face completely changed. His cheeks stretched wide with a grin and grew rosy. He uncrossed his arms and wriggled in his chair.

"Thank you, Cole! And you, too Ms. Yil.... what was your name again?"

"Yilmaz."the artist chirped and grinned. "It's my last name."

"Well, thank you, Ms. Yilmaz. This is awful nice of you."

Yilmaz, Luther thought as he examined her closely. Her complexion was darker that he'd noticed at first; almost middle eastern, but not fully Arab.

"Oh, it's my pleasure Mr. Parker." She turned to Luther, unaware of the dismal storm brewing in his mind. "Would you like a picture, too?"

Her crystal blue eyes contrasted with her Mediterranean complexion and shattered his will to go on about Nimrod and government psy-ops. All at once, under her brilliant stare he realized how insane his words must have sounded, as if they were reverberating in the room and slapping him in his own face.

"Uh…"

Cole smirked. He'd never seen the mighty salesman lost for words.

"He'd love that, Ms. Yilmaz, thank you," Cole patted Luther on the shoulder triumphantly and skipped off to make merry elsewhere.

8

When four o'clock rolled around the only hint of nightfall was the faint glow of the parking lot lights, mostly veiled and hardly visible through the furious snowfall. Luther sat motionless as Ms. Yilmaz scribbled away on her canvas. His blank stare was not at her, for he was too shy, but rather over her shoulder and out the window. The surface of the parking lot had disappeared under the snow. The white lines of the parking spaces were covered, as were the concrete parking blocks at the head of each space. The snow, over two feet deep now, left only a single trail or ditch from the street up to the front door. Every car was covered and unrecognizable. Some would press their key fob while gazing out into the lot, to see if they could locate their vehicle from the quick flash of its lights. But this was useless. Fifty mounds of white powder became less and less rounded as the snow slowly leveled out the landscape. Luther grumbled. Even if the roads were suddenly opened by the authorities, and he was released from the party, he'd have to dig through half a dozen mounds of snow to find his car, clear it off, then clear a path for it to get to the street. He couldn't see the street from his vantage point, but assumed that it was no better - most likely two or more feet of undisturbed and undriveable powder.

How long would this last? How long would he be stuck at the office until the snow was cleared? How much more holiday karaoke could he endure before he strangled Cole and Watts?

As he mused and stewed over his plight there was a sudden movement in the parking lot. A dark shape moved through the cloud of laterally blowing snow. Luther watched as it drifted from behind one vehicle and vanished behind another. Then again. Between the white mounds it moved, across the parking lot and closer to the entrance of the building.

"There's somebody out there," Luther said, keeping his head and face as still as possible. He wondered if the falling snow was playing some kind of trick on his eyes. Perhaps his imagination, ramped up by irritation at being snowed in, was starting to run wild. If it wasn't running wild and there was indeed somebody outside in the middle of their snowpocalypse, would Jenkins let them in? Or would he just hide behind a corner and watch them freeze to death? Luther felt an urge to cut short the caricature artist's process and make sure that didn't happen.What if he was wrong and he left the event hall for nothing? He'd be at risk of being trapped in another gut-turning encounter with the most miserable human being he'd ever met. The janitor was a twisted and mean-spirited creature, and one Luther had grown less fond of. He weighed his options; stay put and risk leaving a man or woman out in the cold to freeze to death, or risk having to listen to the insane bitter rantings of the gnarled old soul emptying trash bins in the lobby.

He went with the former and stayed perfectly still in his chair. It was easy to justify, for anyone who was crazy enough to drive around in a blizzard, or stupid enough, somewhat deserved whatever ill may befall them. *Play stupid games, win stupid prizes,* Luther thought. *Besides, it'd be Jenkins at fault if someone was left out in the cold.* But even as the thoughts were rolling through his mind, his stomach ached with guilt and he squirmed in his chair.

"Don't move," Ms. Yilmaz said, "I'm almost done with you."

Luther's knee started bouncing up and down.

He could hear, over all the noise of the party, five sharp thuds on the main doors leading into the atrium down the hall. Whoever had been wandering through the parking lot had found their way to the entrance of the building and was desperate to get out of the cold. Luther sat motionless. He closed his eyes and strained his ears listening for, hopefully, silence. Surely Jenkins would let the wanderer come in from the snow storm. He wrestled with his body, forcing it to remain still. His knee continued to bounce up and down like the piston of an engine and his gut was doing flips. Several deep breaths didn't help to calm either his physical anxiety or his conscience. But his mind was telling him to just let things unfold on their own. No intervention. *Jenkins' fault,* he thought again. *They should know better than to be out in this weather.... Not my problem to solve.*

Another three loud bangs on the glass of the front doors were enough to pry Luther's eyes open again. This time Rose noticed it over the party's din.

"Did you hear that?" she asked everyone and no one at the same time.

"Hear what?" the cartoonist mumbled as she put the finishing touches on Luther's drawing.

"It sounds like someone is trying to get into the building."

Three more sharp raps on the doors left no doubt that another human being was anxious to get inside. The following moments were filled with a hot silent humming in Luther's brain. He could take no more. He bounced out of his chair and stomped towards the hallway. As he reached the conference hall's exit, a short man suddenly appeared and rounded the corner into the room. Luther plowed into him. A dark blue canvas satchel, which had been slung over the man's shoulder, was knocked to the ground by the impact. Letters and glossy advertisements spilled out into a messy heap.

"Sorry about that" Luther said as he lowered himself to assist in the clean up.

The man, a short hispanic gentleman in his fifties, or possibly sixties, squatted next to him. His postal service-issued coat still radiated the blizzard's chill, and his bucket hat, complete with USPS logo on the forehead, was dusted with flakes still too cold to begin their meltoff.

"No problemo. I just glad de yanniter lemme in."

Luther scooped up the last few pieces of deliverable mail and handed it to the postman.

"I couldn't hear you over all the noise of the party until just now," Luther lied. "Did you say the *janitor* opened the door for you?"

"Si," the postman smiled. "He always' lemme in."

The man looked around the room and slipped off his bucket hat. Beads of sweat dotted his balding forehead, getting caught in the wrinkle across his brow. His mouth curled into a smile, pumping up only one side of his impressive black mustache.

"Do you mind if I seet and take a load off?" he motioned to a chair at an empty table. "I'm stuck in dees bleezzard for a while. Can't get my truck out of de snow."

"Of course," Luther motioned to the same empty table. "Let me get you something to drink."

The man sat down with this bag full of mail on the floor next to his boots. Luther slipped into the hallway to fill up a cup full of sweet tea, while Cole sat down in the chair next to the postman and began chatting with him. The conversation was in Spanish, and was punctuated with bouts of laughter. It was clear that the postman and Cole were already familiar with each other from past encounters, and the easy way in which they conversed gave Luther the impression that the postman was just another perfectly fitting piece to the Christmas puzzle before him. The man was somehow an indispensable part of the whole, not an accoutrement to the party, but a cog that seemed to make it hum along more smoothly.

When Luther returned with the sweet tea, he handed it to the man and asked his name.

"Carlos. Much gusto," he extended a hand. "I seen you many tines up on de turd floor."

Luther took his hand and gave it two firm pumps. "Nice to meet you. I'm Luther Colgera."

"Did you say Colgera?"

"That's right."

The man thanked Luther for the cup, took a quick swig of the sweet tea, winced from its over-sweetness, then set it on the table.

"I have something for you, Senior Colgera. Is een my bag."

He bent down and began rifling through the chaotic heap of letters and mailers. Luther, curious as to what the postman may have brought him, sat down. The jumble of envelopes had been so randomly scooped from the floor and stuffed into the bag only a moment ago that Luther figured he'd be waiting for a while for the postman to find whatever it was he was looking for. But as soon as his butt landed on the cushion of his seat Carlos pulled a small parcel from the satchel. It was the size and shape of a sandwich, wrapped in brown paper with twine tied in a careful bow.

"Thank you," Luther furrowed his brow as he took the package and read the return address.

Terry Street. It was from his parents. The handwriting was his mother's. The light and warmth of the party seemed to dim, as if darkness was creeping into the periphery of his vision. He dare not open it yet; not in front of all these curious people. It was an unwelcome surprise. Though it was not the first time he'd received mail from his parents, it was the first time that he wouldn't be able to fit it in a shredder.

Cole laughed and elbowed him.

"First time getting a Christmas gift, Mr. Scrooge? Are you gonna open it or what?"

The memory of that Christmas with his parents broke back into his mind. The event that had so scarred his heart and drove him from his home and family burned afresh in his memory. He could feel his face flushing and the tension rising in his neck muscles. He'd been trying to forget it for years, pushing the holiday aside as a trifle, hoping that he'd be left alone to pretend it didn't really mean anything so that he wouldn't have to relive his darkest moment year over year. But here it was, in his face once again, this time embodied in an unexpected package and delivered to him... publicly. Christmas had been rammed down his throat. The scab on his heart had been picked off, and the wound bled yet again.

"What's that?" Rose asked. Her enthusiastic flitting about from table to table landed her in the wrong place at exactly the wrong moment.

"It's none of your business," Luther snapped. Before anyone could respond to his rudeness he bounced from his chair and stormed out the door into the hallway.

"Where ya' goin?" Cole innocently asked.

He didn't reply. He was done with the party, his coworkers, Christmas and all. With a loud thud the brown package slammed the bottom of the plastic rolling trash bin.

9

Luther took the stairs and fled the party. He was too enraged to stand in an elevator and wait, even though there were only three floors in the building. He crushed the first flight of steps, taking them two at a time. On the second floor landing he twisted his knee slightly. The pain was sharp and brief, and while it didn't stop his charge up the stairs in the lobby, it did necessitate him stomping on each step to get to the third floor. When he alighted there, he slowed his walk to catch his breath. Nobody in the lobby below could see him. And the sales floor was empty. He was not supposed to be up there. It had been clear that the party was mandatory and that returning to one's desk to work during the festivities was not allowed. Again, he didn't care. *Fire me if you want,* he growled in his boss' face in an imaginary conversation. *I'd be happy to relocate. Perhaps to a place where my parents can't find me.* He had never given his mom or dad, Mrs. and Mr. Colgera, the address of his apartment. He wanted no correspondence from them. Heaven forbid they should ever get his cell number. But even Baby Boomer mothers are clever enough to search the internet and find people. Mrs.

Colgera found his name in a search on LinkedIN. From there a Google search of the company he worked for yielded an address. And so it began. The letters would arrive every couple months or so. They were fetched and delivered to the sales department mail drop by Cole, who'd volunteered to check the mail drop daily in a disgusting act of kissing up to Kondo. Cole picked up the mail daily from the front desk in the middle of the lobby, where an Hispanic postman would make his routine appearance. Luther had never seen the postman, and had no desire for his mail to be forwarded to home address. So he'd resigned himself to sifting through his personal mail at the office, careful to do so over the company shredder. Not a single letter from his parents had ever been opened. If it was from a "Colgera", or had a "Terry St." return address it was treated with more contempt than a political campaign mailer.

He locked the sales floor door behind him, flicked off the lights and collapsed into his swivel chair. His view by the window was normally stunning. A wide panorama of the interstate nearby, and rolling green hills and city scape beyond. But today it was just a sheet of violent snow, visual white noise, up close to the glass and in his face. His neck was sore from the anger that was now abating, and he could feel the day's stress pulling on his mental and emotional reserves. With a twist of a small desk key, and a gentle yank of the file drawer, he removed a small bottle of Kentucky bourbon and a rocks glass. The glass he wiped out with his finger before pouring three fingers of the dark amber booze. Ice was not worth the hassle of juking into the kitchenette only yards away. He'd take it neat. He raised his glass to the blizzard pounding at his window in a salute of surrender, whispering slanders at the day's misfortunes.

"Thought ye weren't supposed to be up here," a cold and raspy voice alarmed him.

Luther jerked from the surprise, spilling a finger of bourbon on his white button up shirt. Before he could wipe it off and turn around to face his rather rude intruder, Jenkins hobbled slowly over to his desk. He emerged from the darkness into the grim light from the snowstorm.

"You scared the crap out of me." Luther was only half exaggerating.

"Hmph. Suppose I'll have to clean that up, too."

"I thought I was alone. I need to be alone for a minute."

Jenkins snickered, "I'm surprised ye didn't give 'em all the finger hours ago. If it were me, I'd rather shove my own face through that window than be at a Christmas party."

"What are you doing up here, Jenkins?" Luther asked with overt annoyance. "The party, and its mess, is in the conference hall."

"Ain't that where *you* are supposed to be? I recall it being, oh what was that word ya used... oh yeah, mandatory."

The salesman sighed and took his first sip of liquid escapism.

"I just needed a break. And a drink." Luther fingered his glass nervously before taking another swallow. "You won't say anything about me being up here will you? And I'm pretty sure I'm not supposed to have this at work..." he pulled another empty glass from his file drawer and poured two fingers of bourbon into it.

Jenkins smiled in his sinister way, more of a half snarl. He slowly blinked and glanced at the extra glass of bourbon.

"Oh, my silence is definitely for sale." He snatched the glass and swallowed the entire pour in one quick gulp. "Thank ye. I'll have another if you don't mind."

It wasn't a request. Luther obliged, and just to take the edge off Jenkins' power move he nodded to Cole's empty swivel chair.

"Nah. Pull up a chair. It's bad manners to drink on your feet."

The janitor rolled up the chair, brushed off some invisible dust, and slowly descended with an air of control and superiority. Oddly, he kept it slightly behind Luther's and off to the side, too distant to convey any camaraderie. They watched the whirlwinding sheets of snow in silence, sipping their bourbon with a snail's cadence. Luther could feel the beady black eyes of the janitor boring into the back of his head. It was so awkward that he had a sudden desire for a karaoke Christmas carol to erupt and brighten the room. That might deter the dark and strange attention he was receiving, and the weird pernicious vibes that radiated from the twisted old man. Finally, Luther shattered the quiet.

"Did you happen to let that postman in the building a little while ago? I heard him banging on the door."

"Of course I let him in!" Jenkins grunted, disgusted at the question. "Who do you think delivers the paychecks?"

"Right."

"It's not like he's some stranger, or some homeless bum. That postman comes by every day."

"So does Winston Watts," Luther replied. Jenkins kept silent and took another swig of bourbon.

"Cole tells me you locked him out of the building..."

Jenkins snickered, "Accidents happen."

"He said that you looked at him after the door latched and rolled away as he tried to get back in."

The janitor stood to his feet. He leaned forward puffing out his chest in and sneered.

"And?"

Luther's fear instinct flickered. The adrenaline began to flow, making his neck feel sore. He suddenly saw the bigger picture - alone on the third floor with a crazy old lunatic, half drunk and irritated.

"He said he offered you a light and shared a smoke. Just seems like a rude way to thank a man."

Jenkins, tense from something boiling deep in his broken old mind, pointed to the floor directly below him.

"I don't owe nothin' to nobody'. And I don't care for your accusations, neither..."

"Easy! Easy. I'm just passing along what I heard." Luther said in a low, and obviously forced calmer tone. "Watts was pretty upset when I finally let him in the building, and cold. Maybe he just didn't read the situation accurately."

Jenkins rolled the swivel chair back to its desk.

"I'd say that he didn't. Bah! I should've let 'em freeze to death with all the other bums in this city." Jenkins topped off his third pour. "You know what, this blizzard is just what we need to deal with the homeless problem around these parts."

Luther agreed that the homelessness in the city was untenable. At least that's how the local talk radio guys described it. And it seemed true. There was a homeless man or woman at almost every intersection between his apartment building and the office. His commute was one awkward stop light moment after another. Through the double glass of his car window and sunglasses, he both watched them closely for his own safety, and ignored them in the same moment. The sunglasses made it easy to look at them without them knowing it, so he assumed. He wondered briefly how one might survive such a snow storm as this being homeless. Where did they go? What if they couldn't get there? And while he didn't really concern himself with the problem beyond complaining about it, he was absolutely certain that Jenkins would shut out, and indeed gleefully shut out a homeless person even in, and especially in, a blizzard.

"Surely you wouldn't let someone freeze to death just because they were homeless... not in a blizzard."

Jenkins face contorted slightly. Even in the unlit room Luther could see the creases forming a 'v' over his old sunken eyes. His bony cheeks, now rosy from drink, stretched the skin from his protruding chin and accentuated his thin drooping nose.

"If God sees fit to cleanse us of the riff-raff, who am I to get in the way? Let the blizzard do its work."

The tongue was thickening in his mouth and the old man slurred every word. He wobbled a bit, then thought it better to sit back down. But before Jenkins could pull the swivel chair back from its desk, Luther made his move to escape.

"Well, Winston may not be the sharpest employee at Blackstone & Harding, but he's a good guy. And he's no bum." Luther took the two now-empty shot glasses and put them back into the file drawer. He locked it up and slipped the key in his pocket. But the half full bottle of bourbon he handed to Jenkins.

"Happy Nimrod's Day," he snarked.

Jenkins barked at him.

"Throw it away yourself!"

Luther, unsure how even this bitter drunk old man could have misread his intention, raised the bottle up towards him again.

"I don't want you to throw it away. It's still half full. I want you to take it and enjoy it."

Jenkins snarled and looked away in spite, but only for a moment.

"It's a gift," Luther sighed. When the old man didn't receive it, Luther gently set it on his desktop and exited the sales floor. He glanced over his shoulder before the door shut behind him. The janitor was rolling his nasty old cart away into the lonely darkness, stumbling behind it slightly. And the bottle had disappeared from the desktop. As Luther descended the three flights of steps, he resolved to return to the party and obey company orders like a good little soldier. There would be no more leaving the party, and God willing, no more chance encounters with the janitor.

10

When Luther returned to the party there was little fanfare about it. In fact, his leaving had been so uncomfortable that most people avoided eye contact. It was awkward. He could sense that he violated something, a social trust. Losing his cool and storming off had put people on edge. He felt lousy about it, too. Fortunately, Watts had kept the mood cheerful as best he could by putting on some Christmas tunes. There was no karaoke happening at that moment, which Luther was grateful for, but the sounds of Bing Crosby and Nat King Cole kept people in the spirit. Most people had helped themselves to dessert and were sitting all about the room, some at the tables, others in chairs formed in a circle, and others in groups on the floor.

Rose was finishing a piece of pie and chatting with Kara, which as it turned out was the caricature artist's first name. They were sitting on the floor, like school children. When Rose spotted Luther awkwardly looking for an inconspicuous place to sit, she waved and motioned for him to join her and Kara on the floor. He slinked over to them, head hanging and avoidant of eye contact with anyone else. He sat down and crossed his legs. Rose beamed at him like a wise and forgiving parent, as if nothing had happened, as if he'd not growled at her and stormed away. Kara smiled at him. A sensation of warmth tickled his gut, an unfamiliar feeling. It occurred to him that this was a first. It was the first time he'd been invited into a small circle of friends, into the confidence of people he barely knew. This was a friendship of sorts, yet one budding during his own inner crisis. This was no fair weather friendship, but a friendship offered when it mattered the most. He sat down with them, joining them with a level of social credit unearned, but graciously given. He knew not why. But it felt great.

"You dropped this earlier when you left," Rose said. She handed him the package from his parents.

He recoiled by instinct, but only briefly. Shame stabbed at him. *I made a real spectacle of myself,* he thought. Then he looked on Rose's face. She was older by at least two decades, and had adult children of her own, possibly grandkids. And while he felt a maternal affection for her, he couldn't shake the image of his own mother's face hovering like a vapor over Rose's countenance. He blinked with effort, shaking the image from his mind, and gently accepted the package.

"Terry Street?" she asked. "I used to know some people in that part of town. They went to my church.

Luther didn't know what to say. Her familiarity with his upbringing, at least in the sense of locale, made him feel connected to her in a new way. He felt they shared roots of some kind. It felt like family, or what he assumed family must feel like.

"You should open it!" Kara chirped.

"I... really don't think I should," he replied. He was terrified of what may lie within, what explosion of angry words, what torments, or twisted memories the contents may elicit.

"Well if you open it and don't like it, whatever it is, you can give it to me and I'll find a home for it."

Luther looked at Rose, now pliable to her influence as well as to the influence of other new found friends. *Oh, what the heck. Why not open it? My parents are dead to me anyhow, right?* He thought. He carefully cut the tape sealing the ends of the brown paper package. He noticed how antsy his friends were when he deliberately slowed down the unveiling. He removed the paper in one untorn and complete piece, and set it aside. The package was made of a small flat box no wider than a postcard, and a letter of the same dimensions on top. 'Luther' was all that was written on the envelope. He quickly slipped the letter into his pocket without reading it. *I'll shred it later,* he thought, *when my friends aren't watching.*

"No need to get all sentimental with private letters and such," he told the two ladies. "Let's see what this is..."

He removed the lid. Inside on a soft pallet of cotton was a silver Christmas tree ornament. It was in the shape of a star and tarnished from decades of display. Within the center of the ornament was a quarter-sized opening with a photo from his childhood, covered with clear plastic. His chest ached and his throat tightened. He squeezed the droplets at the corners of his eyes, forcing them back into their ducts. A flood of grief pounded at his mind's door; grief from the happy days of his youth. It was a time when they were poor, yet he was unaware of their poverty. All he remembered was the twinkle of the lights, the hot chocolate, and shreddings of wrapping paper. The photo was of Luther at ten years old, standing before their tree in the living room. He wore an obnoxious yellow sweatshirt with a Snoopy imaged on the chest. In his arms was a Nintendo, the classic gaming console, still in the box. The smile on his face practically split the photo in two, and standing behind him was his father. One hand on Luther's shoulder, the other holding a mug of steaming coffee. His smile beamed just as brightly, though the enormous eyeglasses distracted from his natural good looks.

"Aw! Is that you?" Kara Yilmaz teased. "You were adorable."

Luther blushed a bit, then replaced the lid, snatching the ornament from their sight. He didn't know what to say. He was walking an emotional tightrope. Oddly, his anger wasn't towards his parents specifically, but for all the Christmases ruined, missed; at himself for holding onto a grudge beyond decency, never even communicating with his own mother. He had an urge to get away from the moment. He needed another cup of sweet tea, or gulp of winter air. Something. Anything other than the oppressing stifling atmosphere of the party. He started to rise to his feet.

"Alright guys and gals," Director Blankenship announced. He'd grabbed the karaoke microphone and hopped up the first step of the dias. "Cole has suggested, and I think it's a good idea, to have another gift exchange. Since we're stuck here with each other, let's have a little more fun. This time we're playing Dirty Santa."

Direction was given to have forty or so chairs once-again arranged in a giant circle. All who had received a gift from the first exchange earlier were to take a seat. Luther, at first, had zero intentions of participating. From the moment he read the email days earlier he'd resolved to skip everything at the party but the food. Now his resolutions had shifted slightly - avoid Jenkins at all costs, and not lose his cool in front of his coworkers. With a gift in hand he really didn't want, he was now resolved to rid himself of it. And the impromptu gift exchange was a perfect opportunity.

All the employees of Blackstone & Harding rushed into action. The circle of chairs was organized in short order and people piled their gifts in a large heap in the middle. Luther placed the little white box on the tip top of the highest stacked gift. And he did it last of all with a bit of flare. Surely someone would be curious enough to snatch a gift brought by Luther Colgera, the one man who rarely participated.

"I'll go first," he volunteered after all had taken their seats. Many were surprised at his enthusiasm to begin the affair, others were suspicious. But nobody objected. Luther stood up and walked to the pile of gifts and selected his own.

"You can't pick your own gift, Colgera," Watts announced. "You'll have to take someone else's. But you can always swap when it's your turn again."

Luther grumbled to himself, something about stupid Christmas, and childish games. He placed his small box back on the pile and took a different one the size and shape of a shoe box. He returned to his seat and opened it. Inside was a strange device - it looked like a severed zombie hand with fingers spread out and curled. There was a wooden knob where the wrist should have been and the tip of each grizzly finger came to a sharp point covered by tiny plastic beads. Clearly this gift was something Justine would have at her desk, and only Justine would wrap a Halloween-style zombie's hand in colorful Christmas paper.

"What is it," Luther looked at her across the circle at her.

Justine beamed with pride. "It's a head scratcher."

Luther placed it on his head and gave a quick test run for all to see. It was heavenly, he had to admit. But as much as he liked it, he knew that it would get swapped by someone at some point in the game.

"Don't get too attached to that Zombie hand, Luther," Cole snarked. "I may be coming for it when it's my turn."

Next up was Kara who had rather conspicuously taken a seat next to Luther. Her immediate presence pressured him to play along with the group. He liked her, or something about her at least though he couldn't quite describe. Her eyes were of course strikingly blue, and that was hard not to notice and admire. But she had a way, a gently imposed compassion and curiosity for others. Luther felt like she cared, though she knew nothing of him beyond the fact that he was once a boy who got a Nintendo for Christmas, and was a bit of a Scrooge during the holiday. Kara bounced up and grabbed Luther's gift from the pile. When she sat down and opened it, she held the ornament high for all to see. A big deal was made by her about how beautiful the 'vintage' ornament was and how nice it will look on her tree.

"Is there a picture already in it?" Oslo asked from across the circle.

"Just a generic stock image of some kid," she replied, while looking at Luther and smiling.

Generic. Stock Image. A kid, Luther thought. *That's what she thinks of me?*

Unfortunately, every gift opened thereafter was way more interesting or valuable than Luther's ornament sitting in Kara's lap. Nobody traded for it. Though the zombie hand was quickly snatched away from him, by Cole, as promised. Towards the end of the game Luther was left holding a set of tacky Christmas hand towels, and Kara Yilmaz was still holding onto the relic from his childhood. He knew that she planned to return it to him. He knew he'd refuse her, and he also knew he was too weak to resist her if she employed those blue eyes in the argument. Finally, it was Rose's turn. She unwrapped a copy of *A Christmas Carol*, by Charles Dickens. There was a quick exchange of glances between her and Kara, then an exchange of gifts. Luther watched his ornament change hands, and while he was glad to be rid of it he still suspected Rose was going to try to return it to him as well. After his outburst earlier, it would be impossible for him to refuse her. Watts was the last to take a turn. He took the Dickens from Kara and the game, Luther assumed, was over.

"Round two," Cole announced.

Luther grit his teeth in irritation. It was just like Cole to have some obscure modification to a game that only an overly-social party animal knew about. But everyone else seemed to know about the strange rule and didn't appear to be opposed at all. It dawned on Luther that they must do this every year, and that if he'd participated even once in the past he'd be savvy to Christmas sub-culture and its morays.

The second round began with Luther, who thought *A Christmas Carol*, while a boring read, was a better gift than hand towels. So he swapped, handing the towels to Watts. According to the rules, one was not allowed to immediately tradeback. Watts was stuck with the hand towels. The next person decided to keep their gift, the next traded gifts. On and on it went until finally, it came to Rose's turn. With another knowing glance at Kara, which Luther was getting rather good at noticing now, she announced that she wished to trade the ornament for *A Christmas Carol*. This move was legal according to Cole, the self-appointed arbiter of all obscure party game rules, since the start of a second round resets everything. Before Luther could protest, the book was snatched out of his hand and the ornament was dropped in his lap.

Luther fumed. He'd suffered two rounds of so-cial-nonsense, chit-chat, and anxiety only to fail at rid-ding himself of the gift his mother had sent him, in his mind *forced* on him. Still there were a few more people who had not taken their turn and the game had not yet ended. *Maybe I can sweet talk them into a trade*, he thought.

But the second round ended in short order, with no one interested in stealing his ornament, and the game was over. There was no 'round three'. Folks were stuck with what gifts lay in their laps, and Luther's prize was the childhood ornament he'd tried to discard.

Once again, Cole took the stage. With a slight twist he amped up the volume on the karaoke machine. He grabbed the microphone and handed it to Watts, who was loosening his collar and necktie.

"Let's all do some caroling, shall we?" he asked the group. It was more of a statement than a request, but none objected. The music began bouncing through the room, the intro to a monster hit, the 1942 *White Christ-mas*, made so popular by Bing Crosby. Watts was no Bing, yet his British accent covered a multitude of vocal sins. It always did. He had social latitude due to the buttery deep timbre of his voice, and the intelligence it, sometimes falsely, conveyed. Watts was a shipwreck of a man, in Luther's opinion. Single not for the first time, he lived alone with his dog, made a sport of hitting on women decades his junior in coffee shops, and collected paraphernalia from the golden age of film making. He was a failed crooner, relegated to using his inherent charm and vocal prowess to sustain himself through a phone sales position.

But when Watts took the microphone it was magical.

"I'm.... dreaming.... Of a white.... Christmas..."

Forty-seven voices joined along in chorus.

"Just like the ones... I used to know..."

Luther looked around to see his coworkers swaying in their chairs, smiles on every face.

"Where the tree... tops glisten... and child...ren listen... to hear... sleigh bells in the snow..."

Luther found his own lips moving as he glanced at the old tarnished ornament in his hands. As he looked at his ten year old self in the photo, he wondered where the joy had gone. Why did adulthood have to be so glum? What happened to all the dreams that boy in the photo had for his own life? Why did that have to die? What would it be like if he never lost those dreams?

As the song progressed, he felt a twinge of sorrow. He had ruined that little boy's prospects. He had crushed that boy's hopes. He'd made a mess of things.

"I'm.... dreaming.... Of a white.... Christmas..."

Watts continued to croon, now amplifying his gestures, and leaning into the performance. Cole, attracted to the attention and caught up in the collective moment, lept upon the stage and directed the crowd. He waved his arms like a conductor, unwilling to allow simple bystanders to simply standby. Participation was required. It must be. This was Christmas, and they were all in this moment together.

"With every Christmas card... I write..."

Luther was singing fully now. Perhaps it was because he could do so and his shabby singing voice still be drowned out by all the others. Perhaps he was growing tired of resisting Cole's nonstop pressure to join in. But when the words *'Christmas card I write'* flew from his lips, he recalled the unopened letter his mom had sent with the ornament. His inner jacket pocket, where the envelope remained hidden, seemed to grow hot.

He resolved to open the letter and deal with whatever it may say.

"May your days.... Be merry.... And bright...."

More than resolve now, he felt an urge to read it, but he could not do so without being alone. It was not the right time to sneak off. Perhaps later. After the caroling was done and people split off into their cliques or turned their attention to chit-chat.

And that was the moment the power went out.

The building, the street lamps, the entire city block, went dark. The karaoke machine popped, and silence pulsed the room and most people's voices were cut off from the surprise.

But not Watts'.

"And may all... your Christmases... be white... "

Luther glanced out the tall windows. The blizzard in full force seemed not so menacing. The sheets of white driving snow were still mesmerizing. Watts began the song over, acapella. He stepped down from the dias as he sang, belting loud the words to *White Christmas.*, and walked towards the windows. Cole followed, beckoning the entire company. By the time they'd sung the song in its entirety they were all standing at the window together, in the light emanating from the falling snow. They stood like door-to-door carolers, enjoying the moment with a cultish glee - as door-to-door carolers often do. Even the postman had joined them, standing next to Luther. When the song ended nobody moved. There were a few peaceful silent seconds, then...

"Silent night..." Rose requested the next song by simply singing it out loud.

Luther had not experienced such tranquility in his adult life. He clutched the ornament. He remembered suddenly what it felt like, way back during the Christmas Eves and Christmas mornings of his childhood.

"Holy night..."

It washed over him, the mysterious joy and serenity of the holiday. The warming glow that everyone expects each year, and marketing companies place all their bets on. But this was how Christmas was supposed to feel, though he'd not allowed himself to feel it for a long, long time.

"All is calm... all is bright."

With all the lights out, the parking lot was more visible. Cars were mere mounds of snow, and everything was blanketed in white powder. The wind was still stiff and biting, blowing eddies off the tops of the cars, and sweeping chaotic swirls along the ground. Luther didn't see how the situation was either 'calm' outside, or 'bright' with the power out.

"Round... yon virgin, mother and child..."

Something moved in the parking lot. A dark heap of clothing wrapped around a wretched figure.

"Holy Infant so tender and mild..."

It was a homeless man. He stumbled from behind one snowy mound to another. Each laborious step brought him closer to the building.

Luther pointed to him.

"Hey. Who's that?"

The caroling stopped. Watts and the Postman leaned closer to the glass.

"He looks homeless," the postman said with an air of sympathy.

"He'll freeze to death." Watts said. "We've got to help him."

If God sees fit to cleanse us of the riff-raff, who am I to get in the way? The thought floated through Luther's mind. He didn't know why the janitor's words were on deck in his mind just then. *Let the blizzard do its work.* Luther recalled also that while Jenkins had let the postman in during the blizzard, he intentionally locked Watts out in the cold. He was a sick man, the janitor. And at the moment he was wandering around the building half-drunk and unpredictable. Luther had no doubt this homeless man was done for if Jenkins had anything to say or do about it. He would definitely be left to face death. By the time these thoughts had run their course through his mind Luther was already sprinting out of the event hall towards the entrance in the lobby. Carlos the Postman was right behind him. If they could get to the doors before Jenkins there was a chance they might save the homeless man without the janitor even seeing it happen.

11

Don't let the door close behind me." Luther gave the order to the Carlos, who nodded. He shoved the door open and stomped into the darkness. The homeless man, poor beggar that he was, had fallen to his knees. The snow was three feet thick at least. When the man stumbled, it looked as if he'd fallen face first. Luther feared he might be too late; that the deep cold had finally seized the man's heart, or at least his will to take another step. But Luther's resolve was to bring that man into the building, even if he had to drag his frozen dead body. Step after cold step, Luther stomped ahead. He'd been outside for only seconds and already his feet were wet and stinging from the bitter cold, drifts of snow falling into his loafers and soaking his thin dress socks. Only seconds, and he was ready to get back inside. The poor old homeless man had been out here for who knows how long. As Luther got closer, the mound of filthy clothing moved slightly. The man raised his head. When he saw a handsome middle-aged salesman in a sport coat stomping towards him, he reached out his hand for help. This was not the panhandler's typical gesture. This was the expression of humanity grasping for life. Luther grabbed his arm and without saying a word, flung the man's arm over his shoulder, stepped alongside him and raised him to his feet. Luther reached his other arm around the man's waist and guided him back through the chaotic ditch of snow he'd just plowed to get to him. They went slowly. Luther directed the man to step in the footprint he had left seconds earlier, footprints that were already beginning to disappear.

"It's a good thing we saw you through the window," Luther grunted as they worked towards the glass double doors.

The man didn't reply. He couldn't. He was already beginning to collapse from the fatigue. When they reached the doors, the postman was holding the door open with one arm. The other door was being held wide by Justine, who'd thrown herself into the action. They both grabbed hold of the homeless man, holding him up as they guided him back to the event hall.

"Grab that chair," Justine barked as they entered. Rose was already in motion, rushing a chair from the gift exchange circle to the table nearest the entrance. They eased the old man into the chair, his clothes were soaking and chilled. Bits of torn fabric here and there were already frozen. The beanie on his head, full of tears and holes, was a cap of ice. Justine gently removed it.

"We need some lukewarm water," again she gave an order to no one in particular. Watts grabbed the hand towels he had been stuck with during the gift exchange and dashed to the restroom. In a moment he returned. The towels were run under warm water and wrung out.

When they placed them on the man's head, color began to come back into his dirty face. He then sighed in a way that was almost a cry of joy. The clumps of snow in his ratty beard were melting off and the muscles of his face were coming alive again.

Someone suggested that his feet be checked for frostbite. The entire company was buzzing with excitement and everyone ran here and there to aid in bringing this frozen man back to life. Luther whispered to him.

"I'm going take your shoes off, sir. I'll be gentle." He'd heard somewhere that nurses and doctors always tell their patients what's going to happen before doing it. It seemed like a rule that deserved following given the situation. The old man simply moaned. Luther carefully removed a pitiful boot, a boot so filthy and disintegrated from wear that it was barely recognizable as footwear. He braced himself from the sight and smell, guessing that neither would be pleasant. But there was no smell that caught his attention or seemed out of place. He slipped the boots off and underneath, the old man had two sealable sandwich bags, the gallon sized, on each foot. The thick plastic had kept out the moisture from the snow, though not the cold itself. The socks on the man's feet, three layers of old knee-highs, had done enough to keep frostbit from setting in, at best as Luther could tell from the dim light, but the man's feet felt like blocks of ice.

Oslo Parker rose from his chair and announced that he had an idea. He waddled out into the hall. He returned a moment later with the punch bowl from the hallway. He had dumped the remaining punch down the drain in the restroom, rinsed and wiped out the bowl, and refilled it with warm water. Kara knew Oslo would struggle to kneel down and get back up, due to his bad knees. So, she gently took the bowl and placed it at the old man's feet. Luther placed one foot at a time in the warm water. A smile flickered over the homeless man's face, and for the first time his eyes opened.

This was a moment of celebration. He'd come back to life in a way, opening his eyes to see the faces of kind people, all decked out in tacky Christmas sweaters, surrounding him and cheering his well being.

"I'll bet you're hungry," Luther said. The man smiled and nodded. Cole had already filled a plate with food, still hot from the Sternos. Watts followed with a cup full of sweet tea and plasticware.

The man was invigorated as he ate. He didn't gorge himself as if he'd been starving. He didn't eat like a pig or a puppy. He placed his napkin in his dirty lap, and held his plasticware with grace. There was an air of dignity about him, though not a hint of arrogance. He would answer questions gently and succinctly. His name was Tom. He was sixty-four years old. He was halfway to a local shelter called Hands of Healing, when the blizzard hit. Luther kept asking him simple questions. He was fascinated by this stranger. He had helped save him from a certain death and wanted to know all about him. But his questions were shallow, like he was gathering the specs to a new automobile he'd acquired. Tom's dignity caught onto this and gave short, tight-lipped answers, which after a while, frustrated Luther. Rose eventually joined the conversion with questions of her own.

"I'll bet this isn't the first Christmas you've had during a blizzard," she said.

The Old Tom smiled, dabbed the corners of his mouth and placed his napkin on his plate. "No ma'am. I've seen worse weather during the holiday, for sure. This is however the first time I've been caught off guard and almost met my Maker.

"How long have you been unhoused?" Justine asked.

"Is that what they're calling it these days? *Unhoused?*"

Justine blushed. "Some people feel 'homeless' is an offensive term. I didn't want to offend..."

Tom laughed.

"I've been *homeless* for fifteen years. And I like to call it what it is. *Homelessness.* I don't have a home. It's not just a house that I'm lacking in my life. It's home. I had both at one time. A nice little place in Tusla. Wife. Couple of great kids... Takes all three to have a home. *Unhoused* is such a ridiculous term. Politicians love it, though. It implies an easy solution, a solution fixed by money. If we can just get more 'affordable housing' - that's their term for cheap slums you see - the problem will go away. The homeless will go away. But men like me don't need houses so much as we need purpose. We had at one time, at least I did. My family was my life, my purpose. They were..." his voice crackled and the lump in his throat choked off the rest of his thought. He took a small sip of his sweet tea.

"It was some life, I'll tell you."

Luther held his breath. There was a story there, a story he yearned to hear. But to ask such a personal question seemed almost like an intrusion into someone's sacred space.

"Tonight," Tom continued, "I was homeless, houseless, and shelterless. My goodness this food is delicious. Is this from Texas Rib House?"

Justine laughed. "You nailed it."

"Thought so. It's like an old girlfriend, or a great ball game. Some barbecue you just never forget. Anyway, I was really in a bad way tonight. What's your name, son?" he turned and looked Luther in the eye for the first time.

"Luther Colgera."

Tom grabbed Luther's hand and squeezed. "Luther, eh? Well, thank you Luther. I owe you for dragging my old frozen ass out of that blizzard."

They chatted some more and Luther asked Tom to tell his story. The old man opened up to them and slowly began to unfold the tale of his life. It started with the picture of a quiet normal life; happy and full of hope. Marriage and children. These made Old Tom light up when he'd talk about them. He said little about whatever it was that he did for a living, to care for his family. Eventually he got to the interesting part, the part where things began to crumble. A drinking problem here, a spat with his wife there. A trip to rehab. While he was in rehab, he explained, and his voice lowered with his bushy eyebrows, his wife and two precious children died. Killed by, of all things, a drunk driver. From there it was a series of blackouts, shelters and programs. Tears streamed down his dirty face. Luther noticed that those nearby, which was pretty much everyone, had gathered around and were also holding back their own tears.

Luther expressed his sympathy with words that felt hollow, untrained, and useless. Others did the same. But their words sounded much more comforting and experienced in grief. Beyond that, one by one, the employees of Blackstone & Harding, Co. began to offer Old Tom the gifts they'd exchanged only an hour ago. The old man, in his great dignity, tried to refuse them. But in the end the benevolent hearts of the blue haired liberals, the meek and mild, the obnoxious and overly-socialized conservatives, all won him over. Luther clutched his ornament in his pocket. He wanted to join in the moment of giving, but what use could a homeless old man have with an ornament from another man's childhood? So Luther searched his soul for another way he may bless Old Tom.

"When this blizzard blows over, and the roads are clear, I'll give you a ride to the shelter. Or wherever you want to go."

Old Tom, overcome by the generosity of the company merrymakers, wiped a last tear from his eye - one of joy - and accepted Luther's offer.

Luther Colgera felt the glow once again. He sensed something come alive in his heart that reminded him of his childhood, something that might exist the next year, and the next. It was something that could always be there if he ever chose to seek it out. He felt the warming of his soul, and the weight of his own conscience. The letter from his mother burned in his jacket pocket. With the momentum only the high of gift-giving at Christmas can bestir, he decided that it must be opened and read at once.

Luther quietly slipped out of the event hall and headed through the dark hallway to the men's room.

12

The hallway leading from the event hall to the restrooms was pitch black. Luther felt his way, running his hand along the wall. When he opened the door to the men's room the wash from the pathetic emergency light practically blinded him. The light hung above the sink, yet the single stall, just beyond the two urinals, was still mostly dark. He squeezed into the stall and locked it. It was dark, silent, and cold in the stall. Luther sat down on the edge of the toilet seat and slipped the letter from his inner jacket pocket. For the first time ever he opened the envelope. The paper inside was a sturdy piece of high end stationery folded in half. There was no letter head or fancy printing. It was not a card, nor was it a piece of simple white copy paper. He unfolded it and could only make out *Dear Luther* at the top. It was too dark to read the cursive covering both sides of the paper. But it wasn't so dark that Luther couldn't admire the perfection, the flowing script and the sweeping letters. His mom's handwriting was a work of art, and it was art that brought back memories of birthday cards, and Christmas gift tags. It was the elegance of the meek woman who had suffered under the agony of isolation from her child for too long. She, the victim of his resentment, was as considerate, hopeful and beautiful in character as her handwriting was graceful.

Luther dug into his pants pocket and flipped open his phone. The light from the display was just enough to make out the first few lines. He had to read them several times, his mind distracted by the idea that he had destroyed such beautiful letters for years, thoughtlessly and brutally subjecting them to the shredder without even being read.

Suddenly the power was restored to the building.

The lights flickered back on across the entire building, and even from the sanctum of the restroom stall, Luther could hear his friends cheering, and the karaoke, the revelry, churn back up in the event hall. He desired to return to them, but also desired to be alone with his mom's words.

Dear Luther,

I pray this letter reaches you in time for Christmas. I sure hope you are happy and God is blessing you. I never expected that you would ever write back or call. I'm not asking you to. I know that you were deeply hurt those many years ago when you left home on Christmas Eve. We are so sorry, son. Your dad has felt awful for so many years. All he talks about is how he hopes one day you'll find it in your heart to forgive him. And currently, it is the one thought that is giving him enough hope to keep him strong for his treatments...

At this Luther stopped. The words, the tone, the soft pleading were heavy blows to his heart. The tears began to form in the corners of his eyes.

... I'm not sure if you've had a chance to read my last few letters to you, but much has happened in the past year and half....

Luther's head and heart began to pound. His body braced itself for impending bad news. But what did he care? He had decided years ago that he hated his parents. He hated Christmas. So why was this so difficult? If Luther Colgera had determined that his life would go on as if his parents didn't exist, why would he allow himself to feel pity? He paused for a moment. The thought of ripping the letter up and flushing them down the toilet manifested in his mind. It was tempting. But even more tempting was the thought to finish reading the letter. He had to know.

... If we knew where you lived, we would have come to visit you for Christmas. Of course, all I know of your life is the address of the company you work for. Perhaps you don't even work there anymore. But now your dad is in no condition to travel, so it wouldn't do him any good as it's too far advanced...

Luther inhaled through grit teeth, his eyes watering, his brain feeling as though it would burst.

... stage four...

The room felt like it was spinning. Luther bent over placing his head between his knees. Sobs gushed out of him, an irresistible torrent, years of grudges and hard-heartedness gave way, and the floodwaters of remorse made him short of breath. The tears dripped from the tip of his nose and splatted the cold white tiles of the men's room stall.

The air in the room shifted and the noise from the event hall was sharply yet only briefly increased. The door had opened. Luther, choked back his anguish, but his sniffing back all that was draining from his face gave away his presence. He could hear footsteps in the room and the squeak of tiny rolling wheels. It was the rolling maintenance cart.

"Who's in here?" a half-drunk Jenkins bellowed.

Luther could hear the slur in the janitor's words. No doubt he'd had more bourbon. And if a sober Jenkins was mean enough to lock a stranger outside in a blizzard, what was a drunk Jenkins capable of?

"Hey Jenkins," Luther called back. "It's Luther. I just needed to step away for a sec."

"What fer?"

"Well, I had what you might call a biological need." Luther flushed the toilet to convince the janitor that he had legitimate business in the men's room. He then rattled the toilet paper dispenser a few times. Then flushed again. When the pageantry was complete, he left the stall and moved towards the sink. But Jenkins stood in his way.

"Sittin' in the dark, eh. All by yer lonesome little self? I don't believe ya. Who poops in the dark?"

"Just because the power goes out doesn't mean my body stops doing it's thing. Where else am I supposed to go?"

Before Jenkins could answer, Luther pushed past the old man, brushing his shoulder. He could smell the bourbon in the air, the booze breath. Luther was still clutching the letter from his mom in his hand. He flicked the sink water on and stuffed it back in his pocket. But the janitor observed it all from the mirror's reflection.

"What's that in yer hand?" he barked in a challenging way.

Luther calmly washed up, and replied, "It's just a letter from home."

Jenkins stepped between Luther and the door and faced him square on.

"Izz that why yer eyez are all red? You been cryin'? You zzad you can't go home and zee yer mommy?"

Luther took a deep breath and clenched his fists. Jenkins stood wobbling before him with a smile curling at the ends of his crusty thin lips. Then he hiccuped. His eyes were bloodshot too, but not from grief.

"If you must know, I just found out my dad is dying of cancer. Stage four, apparently."

Jenkins snickered and stepped out of the way. He fiddled with the paper towel dispenser and grumbled over his shoulder towards Luther, who was practically trembling with anger.

"Juz found out, did ya? Don't talk to mommy and daddy much?"

Luther seethed at the jab, though it was well earned. He fantasized about clocking the old geezer across the back of the head and hiding the body in the snow.

"Probably got the jab."

Luther, on the knife's edge of violence asked, "Come again?"

"Zerves him right if he got the Covid vaccine. If yer dumb enough to get the jab, you get what ya deserve, far az I'm conzerned."

And there it was, the true nature of the twisted calloused old man. The harsh judgment, uncalled for, in a moment of immense vulnerability. A stab in the ribs simply for the pleasure of the pain it may cause. Luther felt his rage melt into pity as Jenkins stumbled about his job. When he began spraying the sink and wiping it down Luther glanced at his reflection before leaving. Perfectly tidy blue jumpsuit, and within, a hopelessly lost and resentful soul. Jenkins looked up from his work in the sink. Luther caught a glimpse of the old man's face. But it was not Jenkin's face, but his own!

It was the face of Luther Colgera, aged by three more decades of vitriol.

So real and shocking, Luther stumbled back and bumped into the edge of the door. He tripped on the corner of it as he quickly, almost at a jog, fled from the mens room and his inevitable future self.

13

The sounds of the party, revitalized from the power being restored, called out to Luther. He found himself not walking, but jogging back to the event hall. He moved like a man about to miss a train or a flight. The image of his own aged face in the janitor's reflection was a future he dreaded. There was a new future, a better man, a more hopeful life that began among his coworkers in the mandatory office Christmas party. His heart conquered, he burst through the doors to the cheers of his friends. Happy to celebrate the return of the lights, they cheered it afresh when Luther arrived. At this moment his heart of stone was replaced with a heart of flesh. With new eyes he took in everything. His grief for past Christmases unlived was overwhelmed by gratitude for all that might still lay ahead. And this Christmas, along with the *mandatory* office Christmas party, sparkled and warmed him in a new way. He saw the mirth of his fellow salesmen and the joy it brought the more inhibited and often recluse coworkers. He watched them come out of their shell and find new friends. He saw the blue haired liberals, his political nemeses, sitting, eating, and conversing softly with the dirty old homeless man. Stripped of meaningless political leanings, he now only saw true acts of human kindness and dignity. He saw gameplay not as an annoyance, but a manifold to warm hearts. He heard jokes and sensed them chipping away the anxiety of work, and the gift exchanges drew people together who would never in the course of a year cross paths or strike up conversation before a coffee pot.

All at once, he saw *Christmas*, in all its jolly and benevolent glory. Every wreath of holly with its deep glossy green leaves and popping red berries was a chrysalis of goodwill toward fellow men and the peace on earth that Christmas had always promised. Candy canes, garlands, and snowmen. The shepherd's staffs that hook around the necks of sheep, *our own necks*, he realized, and keep us from falling over the edge of black human hatred - hooks that draw us back into God's grace and kindness to each other once a year. All of it. Snowmen with corncob pipes and eyes made out of coal, reindeer with red noses, and of course, Santa. Oh, Santa! The embodiment of the jolly endearing soul - out of shape, with no sense of style, and concerned only for the well being of the world's children. A bearded stout old biscuit of kindness and generosity. Then there was the manger, and He who sleeps in heavenly peace within it. All of it, all the symbols and imagery of the ancient holiday, washed over Luther with full force and complete victory. He was, as it turned out, quite happy that he now loved the holiday.

Luther turned away from the group only briefly to refill his cup with sweet tea. A pinch of cocktail napkins absorbed the tears that would not stop leaking from the corners of his eyes. Nor could they wipe the trails away down his cheeks. Thoughts of his father and his poor heart-broken mother also filled his cup, and each gulp of tea, mixed with his tears, in a way refilled his own reserves of compassion, almost communion-like.

"Are you okay, Luther?" Oslo Parker placed a hand on his shoulder from behind.

Am I okay, he thought. *Oh, I am so much better than okay.* He removed the letter from his pocket and waved it.

"Yeah, I just heard from my family back home. Got a little emotional is all."

Oslo gave him a puzzled look.

"Tears of joy, my friend. That's all. I promise these are tears of joy."

Luther and Oslo rejoined Old Tom who, still sitting at the same table, was now surrounded by gifts. With few exceptions, each person at the party had given away their item to bless him.

"My friends, I don't need all this stuff! But I know a shelter full of old men like me who would be really happy to receive such things... if y'all could find a couple of bags to put all this in I'll take it to 'em." Old Tom glanced out the window and sighed. "Of course, I'll try to when this storm blows over."

Luther put his hand on Tom's arm.

"Don't worry about that, Tom. I'll give you a ride myself whenever you're ready to go. As promised."

Tom smiled and nodded. He patted Luther's hand and let out a long happy sigh.

Cole, never wanting to let a hot moment simmer, grabbed the karaoke microphone and asked for volunteers for the next round of singing.

"Come on, guys. My voice is getting tired. And surely you don't want to hear me screech out another carol. What about you, Watts?"

Watts was busy playing the best Euchre hand of his life with Rose, Director Blankenship and Justine.

"Toriko Kondo!" pleaded Cole. "You've been kind of quiet the past couple of hours, Boss. Would you lead us?"

Kondo shook his head. "I'm getting my caricature drawn next. I've been waiting all day."

"I'll do it." Luther shouted. The words came out of his mouth before he realized they weren't simply a thought. The room did ever so slightly get a little quiet and awkward. Nobody expected Luther Colgera to volunteer for anything, especially Karaoke. But Cole was gracious enough to not let awkwardness color or dampen the Christmas spirit.

"Ladies and gentlemen," he announced, "give it up for our very own Luther Colgera."

Luther, now committed to the previously unthinkable, stumbled onto the dias and took the microphone. He was more nervous than he could ever remember being. A crowd of forty people stared at him, waiting for something he wasn't sure he could deliver. His stomach swished and burbled. But as he looked at each individual face, he saw people he *knew*, people that he *loved*, and people that deserved a little more of his Christmas cheer than he'd so far offered.

He whispered to Cole to queue up *Have Yourself A Merry Little Christmas.* As the lyrics bounced into view on the tiny screen at the foot of the dias, Luther opened his mouth and began.

His voice was angelic, it turns out. And just for fun he sang the song in his best Sinatra impersonation. A stunned room held its breath and listened. Luther Colgera, the office Christmas-hater, singing a heartfelt carol was more than they were prepared for at first. Slowly, their shock turned to glee. Smiles split faces, and folks sang along, which greatly relieved a bit of Luther's nervousness. In fact, his confidence grew. He sang louder, filling the room with his voice, his enthusiasm fueled by his coworkers who were all singing along. It was thrilling.

Then Jenkins appeared. He rolled through the doors with his little cart, a smug hateful scowl on his face. Luther continued to sing, not letting on that he had noticed. But he had, and he was keeping an eye on the drunk sour old janitor. Jenkins stumbled to the rolling trash bin near the door, holding onto his cart for balance. None of the coworkers were aware of him as their own backs were turned to the event hall's entrance. They were all facing the stage, where Luther had full view of everything happening in that moment, and about to happen in the moments to come.

Jenkins grabbed the rolling trash bin and began to drag it out of the room when he saw the homeless man.

Old Tom was sitting at a table behind the crowd of carolers. He was singing along as well, unaware of the drunkard walking, or attempting to walk, towards him. Luther could see plainly that Jenkins was unhappy at Tom's presence. He recalled the janitor's disgusting statements about the 'riff-raff' and 'plague' he believed the homeless were to the city. Luther nervously eyed him as he stumbled closer and closer to Old Tom. Kara Yilmaz noticed the shifting of Luther's glance to the back of the room. When she turned to observe what Luther may be looking at, she saw only a happy old homeless man and a janitor checking in on them all, doing his job. She turned back her attention to Luther, with a confused look. As Luther continued to sing, now halfway through the second rendition of the song, he nodded towards the janitor, hoping that Kara may take the hint and head over there to intervene if necessary.

And it worked, to a degree. Kara, unsure of why exactly she needed to move near Tom, did it anyway for no other reason than to be helpful. She and Jenkins walked up to Old Tom at the same time, one from each side. But Jenkins was the first to act. He started slurring his insistence that Tom leave at once. Old Tom, recoiled, upset by the janitor's sudden appearance and aggressive language. Luther could hear none of it over the music and the sound of his own voice blasting through the karaoke speakers. Kara was equally taken aback by the abrupt and forceful commands spewing from Jenkins' mouth. Luther could see the stunned look on her face. But it only lasted a moment. She shot back something at Jenkins, a defense for Tom no doubt, and an insistence that he was a guest of the company. Jenkins was in no state to reason, especially with a woman, a species he deeply resented due to his twisted ideas about culture. He waved her away, shooed her off with a curt wave of his hand.

Then he grabbed Old Tom's arm and tried to yank the man off his seat.

Kara, offended at his condescending manner, and fired up enough to do something about it, grabbed Old Tom's *other* arm and began pulling him in the opposite direction.

Jenkins was too drunk to show strength enough to win a tug of war. But he was angry enough to force his will no matter the cost. He stepped forward and pushed Kara's arm away. Old Tom scrambled to his feet in her defense, standing between the janitor and his young friend. Both old men stared each other down. As they wobbled on their feet; one from fatigue, the other from drink.

All of this Luther observed as he nervously belted the final chorus of *Have Yourself A Merry Little Christmas.* Jenkins, still with a firm grasp on Tom's weak old arm, shouted something at him, screamed it. It was all that could be heard over the music. Nobody else in the room knew what was happening behind them up until that moment. However, even if the sound hadn't penetrated the noise of the chorus, even if nobody could hear it over the music, Luther could read Jenkins' lips plainly.

"Get out!"

Get out; the words that thrust him from his childhood home so many years ago.

Get out; the order given him by his boss when he asked for a concession.

Get out; the words that meant the world valued something or someone *else*, and that you - the refuse - must be dispatched.

And now, Old Tom was the soul shaking at the spear's tip of those hateful words.

Luther, still halfway through the last few lines, cast the microphone away and lept from the dias. Shocked coworkers dove out of his way as he plunged through their gathering. He stormed across the room to the back. In a flash he set upon Jenkins. The old drunkard did not see him coming, nor did he hear the singing stop or the microphone smack the floor. The microphone itself landed next to the karaoke machine's built-in speaker. The feedback tone pierced the air and shattered the moment. A confused audience didn't know what to do, between dealing with the sound, or assisting in the unfolding violence of the moment. It was chaos.

Tom tried to defend himself from the janitor's drunken yanks and punches. His old arm was raised above his head and he pushed forward, moving his assailant farther from Kara and closer to the door. Jenkins at first was trying to pull the old homeless man out of the room, but forgot all about that when Tom stood up to him. Now it was about rage for Jenkins, and punishment. Jenkins fired his fists at Tom, and when they wouldn't land square, he hammered them down on the old man's back. By this point people began screaming. Kara tried to intervene but Jenkins's wild swinging arms kept her from having any success. Luther, however, plowed through the janitor's assault, taking a soft blow to the side of his neck, a blow not intended for him, and barely felt. He slammed into Jenkins from the side and both men tumbled to the ground. On the way down, there was the sound of a hollow thump. Jenkins smacked his head against the edge of the folding table as he fell, then again on the floor. Kara and Justine rushed into the fray pulling poor Old Tom from the violence. Luther lay his full body weight on Jenkins pinning him in place. Jenkins, who lay on his chest, face down, did not struggle.

Luther's adrenaline subsided, and suddenly he felt anxious. Perhaps he had accidentally gone too far, and seriously injured this old man. He scrambled off of Jenkins and back away. Justine wasted no time in assessing the situation. With her finger under the janitor's nose she announced that he was breathing. She, with the help of Luther and Kara, rolled Jenkins onto his back. There were only a couple of mild bruises on his face, not much visible damage done.

That's when the snoring began.

Jenkins in his drunkenness slept hard. It was the kind of sleep that forces itself on a deprived man who's neglected it for too long. The snores were comically loud, and signaled that Jenkins would be sleeping in heavenly peace for quite a while. Just to ensure he'd not be a problem, should he wake up unexpectedly, the mighty

Oslo Parker straddled a couple of folding chairs side by side over Jenkins. With the old man stretched out beneath the chair legs, Oslo sat all of his four hundred pounds on both seats and smiled.

"I'll keep an eye on him" he laughed.

Kara Yilmaz could not resist the opportunity to capture the sight, memorializing it in sketch. She set up her easel, and went to work. Cole fired up some more music, while Kondo and Justine tended to Old Tom, who was fine apart from a couple of scratches and a torn coat sleeve.

14

The drunk old janitor slept for several more hours. No doubt his bitter worldview and lifestyle had robbed him of many years' worth of rest. He slept through the reopening of the roads. He slept through the plowing of the parking lot and the clearing of snow from the sidewalks. He slept through the end of the office Christmas party, and through the tumult of the clean up. Tables were collapsed and rolled away by the employees themselves. The chairs were all folded and neatly stacked along the walls in tidy rows. Rose even pulled the vacuum from Jenkins' utility closet and set it to work. The dias was cleared and the trash was all taken out. Kara and Justine even snatched some paper towels and window cleaner from Jenkin's cart and cleaned all the windows. When the old janitor awoke, he did so to find that the people he hated so much, for so many reasons, had done his job for him. They even left him a plate of leftover barbecue with "Merry Christmas" scribbled on a napkin.

Luther had made good on his promise to give Old Tom a ride to the shelter. All the gifts that Tom has received from the cheerful employees of Blackstone &

Harding had been stuffed in a large trash bag and placed in the trunk of Luther's car. On the way to the shelter Tom reminisced of Christmases past, and Luther was particularly interested to hear what the holiday was like before the old man's family had passed away.

"You got kids?" he asked.

Luther shook his head.

"Well, maybe someday you'll know what it's like. I do hope you do have some little Colgeras at some point. There is absolutely nothing like Christmas morning with your own kids."

Luther thought back to his own childhood; the dark brown carpet of the living room mottled with shreds of wrapping paper, the television reruns of *Merry Christmas Charlie Brown*, the smell of the Fraser Fir in their living room, pancakes and toys. It was pretty great as a kid.

"We didn't have much growing up," said Luther. "But I do remember Christmas morning with my parents."

"That's nice."

"It was pretty standard, really. Mom would make breakfast and dad would sip coffee. They'd watch me open my presents and that was pretty much it."

Tom chuckled, "That's how most people remember it until they have kids."

Luther didn't respond. They drove through town, navigating the icy roads and taking their time. After a while Tom, staring blissfully out the window, began to share more about his family.

"After the crash, Christmas became a day of torment. There's nothing worse than sitting alone in your own living room on Christmas morning. No kids. No wife. No tree. Only the shadows of what and who *should* be there but aren't." Tom cleared his throat. "Only the bottle could make it stop. That's where I found my solace. I took to drinking to drive them all off, my kids and wife. They haunted me for years after they died. There wasn't a place I could go or sight I could see that didn't have a memory of them. They were everywhere I looked. And Christmas mornings were the hardest, and on those mornings the only way to chase off the memories, those ghosts you see, was to drain the bottle."

"I'm so sorry, Tom." Luther could think of nothing else to say, and could find no other way to feel.

"But before the crash," Old Tom continued, "Christmas morning was God's own heaven on earth. Like He carved out a little slice of it, and dropped it right in my own little house. Everything just seemed to shimmer on that morning, especially my kids' eyes. Presents, of course, have that effect on kids. But other things too, like the lights on the tree, and the way the lamp light reflected off the surface of my coffee. The light was just, I don't know, *different*. The smell of my wife's shampoo was stronger, too. Heh. The sun was always shining on Christmas day. Did you ever notice that? Sometimes there'd be snow, and other times not, but I can't recall a single Christmas the sun didn't come out. At least, before the crash. And the music coming from the record player was soft and palpable. You could feel the Christmas carols floating in the air somehow. And what's funny about the whole thing," Tom sniffed back a tear, "is that I remember the smell of the fireplace and the warmth of the flames, but we didn't even have a fireplace! That's just my imagination making stuff up."

Tom laughed at himself.

"It's crazy how our minds take our best memories and exaggerate them. Or maybe it's not our minds. Maybe it's our hearts that do that. I don't really know."

Luther felt a pang of conviction when Tom said this. While the old man confessed to the exaggeration of his best memories, Luther realized that he had exaggerated his worst opinions about his coworkers and about Christmas. It was his heart, and not his mind, at fault. Luther squirmed slightly. He was uncomfortable with his guilt, and a change of subject was the only thing he could reckon might distract him from his feelings.

"I used to love Christmas when I still lived at home. But now," Luther explained, "I just see the commercialization of it all. I have a hard time believing it's as special as our memories want to make it."

"Oh sure. It's always been like that though, even when you were a boy."

"Probably true. But have you ever questioned the origins of the holiday?" Luther was hoping for some wisdom that could free him from the ideas the twisted old janitor had planted in his mind.

"What do you mean?"

Luther explained that *he* had heard Christmas was celebrated on the birthday of some ancient Babylonian deity or figure. He explained that displaying a tree inside the home came from some ancient pagan practice.

"It was co-opted by the Christian church. But they didn't remove any of the pagan symbols or change many of the practices. And here we are hundreds of years later acting like it's some Christian holiday. They say it's about the birth of Jesus Christ, and let on as if that's how the whole thing started."

Tom listened patiently as they got closer to the shelter. When Luther pulled into the parking lot, they both sat in his car for a few moments more.

"I believe that Christmas is what you make of it," Tom said. "That's what Christianity did, in my opinion. Sure it's a commercialized holiday. That's what our government and economy has made of it."

"That makes sense, I guess."

Tom smiled and unbuckled his seatbelt.

"The question is, my young friend, what will *you* make of it?"

Luther smiled and said his goodbyes to his homeless friend. He helped remove the sack of gifts from the trunk of his car and handed it to Tom.

"Thank your coworkers again for me. These will make Christmas just a little brighter for all my friends in there," he pointed towards the shelter doors.

Luther felt once again the warm glow of goodwill, as he saw the selflessness of a man who had so little; a man who'd lost so very much, and still loved Christmas as if he were still a child himself.

"Wait," he said as Tom began to walk away. "I have something for you."

Luther slipped the childhood ornament from his pocket and handed it to Old Tom.

"I'm guessing there's probably a Christmas tree in there somewhere."

Tom looked at the tarnished ornament and twirled it slowly in his fingers.

"Is that you and your family in that picture?" Tom asked, smiling.

"It is."

"You still stay in touch with 'em?"

Luther hesitated. Before he could answer, Old Tom discerned there was something painful there.

"After all these years of being away from home, I..." Luther forced a lump back down into his throat. "I need to. It's been years. I'm not even sure how to reach them beyond an address."

Old Tom nodded and went on about how families should always stay in touch. Christmas was the best time of all to heal and reconnect with those we love. Luther had heard all that before, mostly from Hallmark commercials. But now it made weird and profound sense to him, at least to a degree.

"Young man, I lost my family years ago. Wish I had 'em back. And I think this ornament is the greatest gift you could've given me. It's almost like you're giving me the family in that photo. That was very thoughtful. Thank you."

Luther shook Tom's hand.

"Merry Christmas, Tom."

"Tell your parents, Merry Christmas, Luther. I'm certain they'd love to hear it. And have a Merry Christmas yourself."

15

The next two days brought weather just warm enough to turn the world to gray slush. On Friday morning, the last work day before Christmas, Luther breezed into the office with a stack of cards in his hand. He planned to hand them out to those whom he'd gotten to know better at the party. It would be a small gesture, but it gave him a feeling of belonging, and hopefully, it would bless those whom he'd formerly cursed. However, the route to his desk never took him through the main entrance of the office suite. He entered from the back of the suite farther down the hallway. Nobody seemed to be at their desks, but he could hear them all chattering in a large group on the other side of the office, near the main entrance. He thought nothing of it at first and sat down in his swivel chair. Before he could swing around and take in his customary morning view of the highway, he noticed a small package by his keyboard. It was the size and shape of a small book, but wrapped in newspaper. There was also a card stuffed into a red envelope, addressed to him by his first initial and last name.

Luther wondered if Kara Yilmaz perhaps thought enough about him to do such a thing. Or perhaps it was just Cole, who seemed to be the soul of generosity itself, giving gifts just to keep the party going days after it came to an end. He grabbed the package first. The newspaper, he noted, was smudged. It had seen use beyond simply reading. There was a cord of twine around it, tied in an impossible knot. With no pocket knife or scissor handy, Luther resorted to using his keys to saw through it. Eventually he snapped the cord free and tore the newspaper away. The gift was not a book, but a white cardboard box, similar to the one his mother had sent him in the mail. Inside lay the tarnished silver star ornament he'd given Old Tom only two days prior!

Confused, he grabbed the red envelope and ripped the card from it. It read:

Mr. Colgera,

Thank you for the gift of a 'family' this Christmas. A couple of days ago you displayed a deep generosity that makes this truly the most wonderful time of the year. Thank you for saving me from the cold of the blizzard, the wrath of the hateful, and the loneliness of my situation. Speaking of my situation, I must confess that I bent the truth somewhat about that. Sometimes there's really no way to get to know people without disguise. I cannot in good conscience keep your childhood ornament, and would ask that you take it back and cherish it. Anyway, I'm so proud that you represent this company and hope that you'll value my gift to you and your coworkers this year. You'll find your gift on the little Christmas tree at the front of the office.

I wish you a very Merry Christmas.

Your friend,

Thomas Blackstone,

Blackstone & Harding, Co.

Owner

P.S. Jenkins has 'resigned' and will be seeking other opportunities.

Luther hurried to the front of the office. His mind reeled. Every interaction with Old Tom had been based on a lie. Though somehow he wasn't offended. The thought that the very owner of the company disguised himself as a homeless man and visited his own company's Christmas party made him smile. It was an ingenious ruse, and Luther at once admired it.

The entire office was crowded around the little artificial Christmas tree by the entrance. People were leaning over each other's shoulders, fingering the three dozen paper ornaments that hung all over. They were tags, on each a different employee's name was written, along with a dollar amount and the name of a charity. There were oohs and ahhs, and excited yelps when someone found that special tag with their name on it.

Watts had found his tag first, as he was always the first in the office. When he noticed Luther approaching, he smiled in a way that betrayed, intentionally, a secret.

"Mr. Blackstone himself did this. I can hardly believe it."

He handed his tag to Luther for examination. The company had donated five thousand dollars to a veterans organization in Watts' name! The dollar amount on Jeremy Cole's tag was the same, though the charity was different. Each employee's amount was the same, but the charity was something special just to them. 'Old Tom' had done all of his investigation, disguised as a homeless man, while mingling with them at the mandatory office Christmas party. Luther laughed and reeled and wondered. Rose and Justine wiped tears from their eyes, while Oslo stood by the tree shaking his head in disbelief. While the donations were special, the ruse that Thomas Blackstone had pulled hit home the most. Luther felt as though he should kick himself for not knowing what the owner of the company looked like. None of them did, in fact. He was just the name on their letterhead, directing the company remotely from the confines of some dark boardroom high above the clouds.

"Here's yours, Luther!" Rose announced.

Luther plucked his tag from the top of the tree, just below where a customary star or angel would be. It dawned on him just then that his childhood ornament was still clutched in his left palm. He hung it in the tree as close to the tip top as could be done. The act of placing it on a Christmas tree somehow brought the ornament back to life, after years of not seeing it hanging on the tree of his childhood home, it now had meaning again.

He had meaning again.

He stepped back and read the tag silently. His hands began to tremble. His eyes told him what he himself refused to believe. He reread the tag, mouth agape. Fifty-thousand dollars, in the name of Luther Colgera, Sr., Luther's father, had been donated to the Helping Hands Shelter! The script on the back of the tag was a handwritten note.

Luther,

I didn't decide what amount to put on the check until you dropped me off at the shelter.

Thank you for your generosity and love for Christmas.

You gave me the gift of your family, with the ornament.

Allow me to return the favor...

555-236-9871

Luther yanked the flip phone from his jeans. He smashed each number on his phone quickly and hit "call" before he could talk himself out of it. As it rang, he slipped through the entrance of the office, into the hallway for some privacy.

His mother answered.

The first few seconds were nothing but happy sobs and laughter from her. Luther asked to talk to his dad. When Mr. Colgera, Sr. answered, Luther was suddenly at a loss for words. He'd rehearsed an apology several times over the past couple of days, but now nothing would come. The words could not be summoned past the shame and heartache. All he could manage were sporadic mutters.

"Hey Dad... I... Um... Can I come home?"

His dad didn't respond for a few seconds. Luther heard a wet sniff, and the sound of swallowing, then a weak voice, warbling with joy.

"Yes son. I'd love nothing more. Please."

Luther, doing his best to keep himself pulled together, needed to make sure he said what he felt the moment called for, what he had prepared for.

"Dad, I'm sorry for..."

His dad stopped him, "Me too, bud. I'm sorry too. Don't say another word about it. Just come home."

It was Mr. Colgera, Sr.'s last Christmas.

The End.

Acknowledgements

To the fiends and friends at Foundation Group, Inc. who inspired the events and characters in *Mandatory*, thank you. Also, I'd like to express thanks to my wife RaeAnna and my son Christian for the tremendous help in editing and proofreading the manuscript. Their sharp and critical eyes made the book so much more readable. Though I was pressured by my wife to make some sketches for each chapter, I don't believe that my crude drawings would have made the book more enjoyable, and I refuse to use artificial intelligence for such things. MiblArt designed the cover, and I am completely thrilled by their work, as always. I'd like to finally express a heartfelt thanks to the great Steven Pressfield, 'Uncle Steve' - an author who'll probably never read this book, but whose wisdom and encouragement gave me what I needed to push through the Resistance and finish this project.